TUGS O

Once Upon a

by Betty D.

ISBN Nº 0 948204 99 0

Published by Barny Books
PO Box Nº 38, Oxford OX2 6FD
Hough on the Hill, Grantham, Lincolnshire

Produced by: **TUCANN***design&print*, 19 High Street, Heighington, Lincoln LN4 1RG
Telephone and Fax: 01522 790009

Part One
Eastward bound. August 1940

I'd two hours to pack until I had to start my journey for home. Home! What was my home going to be? I'd not been to India since I was tiny and now, suddenly I was leaving school, Aunt Mathilda and all my friends.

I had been sent to England when I was four and had only seen my father, Clive, for four months since then. Would he recognise me and would I know him? I knew I would recognise my mother, Ethel, for she had been back to England for some of the long summer holidays. I had never been to Shillong, on the Assam\Burmese frontier. That strange sounding place was to be my new home.

Emma at the age of 1 in Calcutta

The boat train to Glasgow picked up steam. Aunt Mathilda wept silently into her small lavender scented handkerchief. I had no idea that she cared for me so much. I thought she had looked after me as a kind of family duty. My throat tightened as I bent down to kiss her wet cheeks, the net off her wide brimmed black velvet hat caught in my hair. "Don't cry, Aunt Mathilda. You're the best person in all the world. I'll write to you, promise I will. Lots of letters about what's happening." She gave my hand a squeeze. "Go on, dear, hop in." Her self control came to the fore quickly. "Give my love to Clive and Ethel. Thank them for letting me have you." She turned abruptly and walked slowly away. The train began to move. Aunt Mathilda's small frame disappeared in the clouds of steam. I felt alone and vulnerable immediately.

The country side flashed by. There were no place names at the stations in case of German invasion, so I did not know where we were. I began to feel hungry and peeped into the picnic Aunt Mathilda had packed from her own rations. While I ate I thought about my school life. Clapping, and more clapping as I climbed the platform to collect all my sports prizes. I was good at sport. I thought about my friends, and Diana. She was my special friend, a sort of sister I never had. I felt a tear starting to trickle down my cheek and quickly rubbed it away. I'd always been told it was not done to cry and show emotion and there was I crying for what was now a memory. I hadn't wanted to leave school and go 'home' to India. I'd been in England since I was four. Now that war had broken out, my father wanted the family to be together. I had planned what I wanted to do with my life. I was going to try for Bedford College and do Physical training and Massage. Now all those plans had gone. I was returning to a country and family I could hardly remember. I thought of my parents as Clive and Ethel, the role

Emma's Parents

then of father and mother seemed so remote. I wondered what this strange place called Shillong was going to be like. They'd described their house and sent photos but I'd never thought I would go there to live.

The train stopped at a station. "Must be Birmingham," said an elderly gentleman. A crowd of brown bearded men wearing long shirt-like garments thronged the platform. "Seem to be taking on a load of Sikhs," muttered my companion, "probably earned a living as travelling salesmen, going from door to door with a suitcase of things made in India. Can't have too many foreigners around in war time, so back to India they must go." I watched the Sikhs pushing and shoving and realised I had never seen people like them before. In my life I had only seen white people and only a very few men. I had lived with dear elderly Aunt Mathilda and attended a single sex Boarding School, where boys were never allowed to be mentioned, let alone seen. As light was failing the train drew into the docks. Small ships were moored all along the quay. The elderly gentleman saw I looked perplexed. "Come along, dear," he said. "We've got the same luggage labels, so follow behind." We passed a line of blackened and grimy ships, and soon arrived at S.S.Terne. She was filthy and puffed thick smoke. I struggled up the gangway, bumping the sides, and tried to thank my elderly guide, but he had disappeared.

A man in blue with 'Purser' on his lapel took control. He passed me on to a dark-skinned steward who gathered up my luggage and led me to my cabin. There was a smell of hot oil and cabbages, and the paintwork needed a wash. My cabin companion was a middle-aged woman who smoked, had hard eyes, and grumbled. I knew I wouldn't like her straight away and, after listening to her rantings for a short while, I excused myself. I leant over the railings and felt the welcome night breeze on my face. My thoughts were disturbed by the tannoy blaring, ordering us to do boat drill. A kind lady called Mrs Quinn told me where to go and sympathised with me over my cabin companion whose name was Maude. Maude was well known for her heavy drinking habits and ship board romances. Mrs Quinn tied my life jacket properly and we waited in rows behind an allotted lifeboat. Soon the Sikhs crowded the deck and stood behind us in a forlorn cluster, huge men with sullen faces. They smelt of sweat. Mrs Quinn explained that they were in the bowels of the ship, terribly over-crowded, and with no ventilation. She was not a bit concerned which sur-prised me.

In spite of Maude's snores and smelly cigarette smoke I slept well, but woke early to the rhythms of the engine and swaying of the ship. I dressed quickly and left Maude and made my way to the top deck. It was calm and grey, every-thing seemed grey. I saw a armada of small ships chugging along in rows, keep-ing in formation. A smaller ship, one that was used for carrying bananas and was quite speedy, was moving up and down one side of the convoy. It had one gun on its stern. Our S.S. Tern was on the outside port flank.

I met Mrs Quinn and asked her. "Why are we all in lines? Why are we going so slowly?"

"You see, m'dear, if we're in lines then the U boats won't be able to hit the ones on the inside with their torpedoes. Full of ore, they are, for munitions. Essential for the war effort."

I worried. "But we're full of people and we are on the outside. Aren't people important too? And why are we going so slowly? We'll be a sitting target."

"Got to go at the speed of the slowest boat. About seven knots, I should think." Mrs Quinn turned and left for her cabin.

On the third day out I was sitting by the railings on the front of the top deck. The steward had just been round with hot Bovril. I found the steam and aroma comforting. I watched the ship next in line, its bows were slightly ahead of ours. Large ponderous waves made the bows heave slowly. I looked for the banana boat. Instead I saw a cigar-shaped shadow sneaking through the sea underneath the wave tops.

"What's that?" I exclaimed, as the shark-like object streaked by. There was a shout from the lookout in the crow's nest. A loud explosion shook the cup in my hand. Debris sailed through the air. A piece of wood landed by my foot. Sirens blared. People ran. I sat in my chair frozen with fear. I stared at the adjacent ship, the one I'd been quietly watching. Its bows had been blown off. There was a jagged open jaw instead of a point. Both ships were still moving with the swell. I smelt hot metal. A young seaman passed by. He yanked me out of my chair and chivvied me to get moving to my boat station.

Mrs Quinn was waiting at the appointed place, biting her nails. "You've got it on back to front. Pull yourself together, Emma." She saw I was shivering. I adjusted the bulky life jacket.

The Sikhs appeared. Mumbling and grumbling they stood behind our assembled group. There was another explosion, and the crippled ship disintegrated before my eyes. Our ship shuddered. Flotsam and jetsam floated on large waves, and scraps of metal fell near us. The Sikhs became silent. There was only the sound of our engines.

Maude appeared, dawdling along. "Bloody noise," she said. "Woke me up, it did." Then she saw the scene of desolation. "Christ, what a mess. Must get a fag. Me 'ands shaking. Come on, Emma. Gimme some 'elp."

Two hours ground passed. Murmuring grew. The S.S. Terne moved steadily forward. At last the all clear sounded. It was time for the midday meal but the dining room never filled up. I could not eat so I stood by the rail on the port side. The officers and crew were uncommunicative and busy. Everyone watched the sea as the convoy moved on in the greyness of the day.

At four o'clock that afternoon, a ship, also in the outside lane, suddenly blew up. Alarms wailed again, passengers scuttled to their boat stations. This time the Sikhs had arrived first and stood next to the rail near the lifeboat. I was pushed to the back of the deck along with some other women and children. Maude was incoherent and could barely stand. I looked ahead to where the torpedoed ship had been. There was nothing there, no lifeboats floating, just a few people in the water. When a wave crested I saw heads and arms. Our ship sailed on relentlessly. Save for the swishing of the sea the silence was crushing.

Mrs Quinn looked at Maude with disgust. "She'd be no good in a lifeboat," she said. "That is, if there's room for any of us once the Sikhs have pushed in first."

The thought of sitting in a lifeboat drew my attention again to our present dilemma. It was the quiet that was disturbing once the explosions and calls for help and sirens had died down. We waited five hours, cold and tired. The light was failing when the sirens wailed the all clear. Mrs Quinn helped me lug Maude to the cabin. No dinner had been prepared so I had a hot drink and a peanut butter sandwich. When I woke in the morning I found we sailed alone, even the escorting vessel had left us.

Two weeks later while I was waiting for the dinner gong the tannoy blared. "Attention please. Will all first class passengers return immediately to their cabins until further notice. There's unrest in the lower decks. Hurry up, please. All passengers to their cabins." As I reached my cabin I heard a scurry of feet. A tall dark man rushed past the open door, followed by another. A third man ran after them and I saw a curved knife in his hand. I shut the door quickly, my heart thumping. There was no sign of Maude and I didn't like being alone. There were no more footsteps so I opened my door gingerly and peered down the passage. Mrs Quinn had her door ajar and was peeping out too. She beckoned and I slid quickly into her cabin.

"The Sikhs have mutinied," she said. "They're demanding more air and better conditions." There were more footsteps, then shouts and sounds of chopping. "They're chopping at the railings with those horrid knives. Quite mad, they are."

I shut the porthole quickly. While we waited for the tannoy to make another announcement, Mrs Quinn explained that many Indians came to Europe as traders and that it was unfortunate for these Sikhs that they should be trapped in England at the onset of a World War. Unless provoked, she continued, they were an intelligent tribe using their skills as money makers.

At last the tannoy blared. The trouble was over, and we should all assemble in the dining room one hour later when the Captain would explain the situation. The Captain made a brief re-assuring speech. He said that the Sikhs demanded better conditions. They were to be allowed on the lower deck till 10 p.m. Any more trouble and they would be put ashore at the nearest port. Then he wished us all good night and hoped we'd enjoy the lights of Capetown which we'd soon be seeing.

Excitement grew as the summit of Table Mountain appeared the following evening. Everyone watched the twinkling lights appear as darkness draped itself over the city. It was fairyland. We caught a city smell as we slowly glided into the harbour, a musty, musky smell polluting the purity of the sea air. The S.S Terne drew up alongside. No first class passengers were allowed ashore, even for an evening meal. The Sikhs were allowed on the dockside, but not into the town. It gave them an opportunity to move around. I heard them all through the night enjoying the cool clean air, their coughing and spitting and sudden bursts of laughter making a change from the song of the sea. Clean water and supplies of fresh food were loaded as well as the everlasting tons of coal. Having been at sea a month my eyes feasted on the bright colours of the plants that festooned the whitewashed houses.

We left port at dusk. After dinner I went up on deck. The crew were battening down the portholes and moving the deck furniture into lockers. I anticipated a storm and already felt the exaggerated movement of the ship. For the next three days she ploughed through mountainous seas. She pitched, tossed, rolled and shuddered. The engines never wavered. I never saw the albatross that followed the ship flutter a wing or a tail feather. It seemed sucked along in the ship's vacuum. I was deliriously happy on the deserted deck. I was the only one to brave the fresh air. The albatross disappeared with the storm and the passengers settled into the usual dull routine.

There was so little to do on board, just reading, talking which turned to gossip, drinking and eating. We were told the journey to Bombay should take about three weeks, and although we still had the blackout regulations the chances of U-boat attacks were minimal. Tempers were frayed and grumbles abounded, but Maude could still out complain them all.

When the coast of India appeared slowly far away on the horizon everybody cheered; even the Sikhs let out a howl. I watched as Bombay grew closer and saw large white houses with shuttered windows, palm trees swaying in the breeze lined parts of the water way. Behind the waterfront and creeping up the sloping hills were huts, rows and rows of huts all with corrugated roofs. As we neared our mooring I saw masses of bicycles, cows and goats.

The S.S.Terne made her way to her appointed dock while I watched, soaking in the sights and sounds. Dark people were everywhere, like ants in number. The ship moored next to us was being loaded with coal by an endless chain of men with thin black legs each balancing a basket of coal on pancake-like headgear. The chain never stopped, the black dust came in constant puffs as each basket was tossed into the hold. Everywhere was grimy. I wiped my face and my hand was streaked.

I was packed and waiting when I heard a voice say, "Good morning. I understand you're Emma. Your father asked me to see you safely on the train. I'm Albert Franks, from Bibby's. Where's your luggage, girl? Want to get to customs as quick as poss. Got a lot to do to-day."

I felt Albert Franks was bored with the whole situation. I instantly disliked his large flabby stomach and wet cigarette. He smelt like Maude and he sweated profusely. With help from stewards, porters and a big tip from Albert to the customs officer I was first to arrive at the boat train.

"That's you all fixed up," said Albert with a sigh of relief. "You've got a lady from the ship in this compartment, so you should be safe. Bombay's like a circus now with all the soldiers coming through. Tell your father I did as he asked."

"Thank you for your help, Mr Franks. I'll give my father your message." I held out my hand but Mr Franks was too busy to give me a courteous response. He had turned away immediately, harassed and hurried. I saw him later in the station bar with a tall glass in his hand. He seemed in no hurry then.

The train was much larger than anything I had seen before. Our compartment was small with only two bunks, the top one being hooked up during the day. There was a fan, a lavatory which needed cleaning, and a wash basin. Shortly afterwards Mrs Quinn appeared, made herself comfortable and claimed the lower bunk. I was glad to be rid of Maude.

The train slowly pulled out of the station I sat by the open window and looked out.

"Best you pull the glass layer down, dear. It'll stop the smuts," suggested Mrs Quinn. "At night we pull the wire down, and when it's very hot we use the slats. Got to keep the sun out, you know."

As the train picked up speed, the scenes from the window frightened me. "Look at those children," I called to Mrs Quinn. "That one's got his leg at right angles to his knees. And that girl has her arms above her head and she can't move them. It's horrid."

"Emma dear," interrupted Mrs Quinn gently. "That's how the families make money when they're poor. They maim the child, then collect the money from the begging. It's all some can do."

I turned again to watch the pathetic parade. Small wooden trolleys on bent pram wheels carrying handicapped children were pushed and pulled by others who should still be at school. Older men leant on sticks and held out withered hands. Women with bare empty breasts sat and hugged a crying child. Beyond the straggling beggars the earth was brown and parched, a few trees survived to give shade to some skinny goats. A bullock dragging his wooden-wheeled cart groaned along a dusty track, a young boy at its head.

"It's not like this in Shillong, Emma." Mrs Quinn's voice broke through my gazing. "Good clean air, and lovely flowers. Much better for you than Calcutta."

"That's what my father says. He's done twenty five years on the plains and in Calcutta where he ended up as a Judge. Now he's called the Legal Remembrancer. He sort of administers the civil side of Assam. He'll be in Shillong for some while."

The train slowed down with repeated jerks. "Ah," said Mrs Quinn. "Our first stop for dinner. We eat in the station restaurant. The boy comes in to make the beds while we're out."

When we juddered to a halt, the carriage door was opened by the boy who turned out to be an aged man with grizzled hair. The smell from the platform was terrible. It was difficult to walk to the refreshment room. Bodies wrapped in dirty cloth were lying on the ground. Goats and cows wandered around unattended. Men sold Indian sweets and water from wooden trays balanced on their heads. The Europeans soon seated themselves in the restaurant. I tried for the lavatory but the smell and piles of excreta turned me back.

"What about the others?" I asked Mrs Quinn. "All those people sitting on those wooden benches in the third class carriages. Don't they get any supper?"

"No, my dear," Mrs Quinn said gently, sensing my agitation. "They don't eat or drink on the journey, other than what they can buy through the window. They'd lose their place if they moved."

A plate of grey meat was put before us surrounded by rice. "Lamb stew," Mrs Quinn muttered quietly. "But it's probably one of the oldest goats. Never mind, Emma, try hard."

I tried unsuccessfully with the stew, had better luck with the baked caramel custard that followed, and I really enjoyed the hot sweet tea.

"Come on, let's go before the rush starts." Mrs Quinn was a seasoned traveller and a great comfort to me. "Get to bed quick, before the train begins to shake, and don't forget to lay a towel over your tummy. If the fan blows on you,

9

you'll get the gripes."

Shortly after dawn the train stopped at a tiny country station. The elderly 'boy' bought hot tea with rolls and butter. It seemed like manna from heaven. My mouth felt and tasted like the inside of a birdcage. He left some packets and small bottles of liquid.

"That's for our lunch and tea," said Mrs Quinn laughing.

The rest of the journey passed in a haze. Going to the lavatory was so unpleasant that my bowels became bunged up. I got accustomed to the nightly stew and caramel custard. After three nights and three days we arrived at Calcutta and I said a fond good-bye to Mrs Quinn.

The shouting and fighting between coolies trying to carry the white passengers' luggage frightened me. I had no idea of the ritual. I stood on the steps of the carriage, undecided and nervous.

"Hi, there! Are you Emma?" A tall thin man called out. He wore a toupee, and long khaki shorts down to his knees. Like most middle-aged men I'd noticed, he was red in the face. "Thought I'd missed you. Used to work for your Dad. Come on. We've got to get a move on to get across Calcutta."

Totally unable to act for myself, I followed this thin man. He organised a fleet of coolies, two pieces of luggage to each coolie. We wove our way through people sitting down, people sleeping, and people standing. There were several men with red teeth. They spat a red juice with accuracy to the base of pillars, missing me by inches. How I wished for a bath or a really cool drink.

The thin man hailed a taxi. We piled in, the luggage was stacked around us. "Sealdah," my escort said. The driver rattled off. Everything shook. He drove on the horn. Cows scattered, children nipped out of the way at the last moment.

"We've got to go right across the city," he explained. "This other station has smaller gauge railws. You've another two nights and a day. Bet you could use shower." He gave me a wry grin.

It took half an hour to get to Sealdah. My impressions of the city streets as I peered through the dirty taxi window were of masses of people, people moving, people carrying different things, people on bicycles, people sitting on pavements just looking. The taxi dodged round emaciated cows and scantily clad children. There were shanty huts lining the pavements overshadowed by great concrete buildings. I didn't see many shops. At Sealdah the coolie process was done in reverse.

The thin man found my compartment and got me established. I could see him sigh with relief as he got rid of me. This compartment was smaller, again with two berths.

One berth was already occupied by a young nun who was travelling to Shillong for a rest. "Shillong's seven thousand feet up. The air's wonderful. Most white people try and get there during the hot weather for a rest. You're a lucky girl to have a home in such a lovely place." She was a quiet companion and promised to help me with the coolies when we arrived.

The terminal was a one platformed station adjacent to a vast slow moving river. The nun attracted the attention of four elderly coolies whom she seemed to know. They nursed my luggage off the train, on to the ferry and off again at the far side. The nun showed me how much money to give as buckshi, or tip. Several old buses stood in line. The nun steered me to one marked Shillong, saw my luggage was aboard and left me, saying she was following later. I thanked her profusely and sat in the front seat for the sixty mile drive up a tarmac road to Shillong. The road wound round the contours of the hills which meant a

Emma's father

steep ravine on one side. Hairpin bends had been hacked through thick forests. Creepers and trailers encroached on the road space, banging on the roof. Bright flowers climbed up the tree trunks. The air blowing through the open window was cooler and crisper. My stomach was churning. It was four years since I had seen my father. Would he like me, I wondered? Will my mother be the same as during her visit to England two years ago? What am I going to do all day? These thoughts whizzed through my head as we drove into a large corrugated iron shed. This was the bus station and I was at the end of my journey. What would happen if my parents were not there to meet me?

They were standing near a door marked Exit. My father looked the same as in the photograph I'd kept on my dressing table. He was balder, but the black round glasses still perched on the end of his nose. He wore long khaki shorts, long socks up to the knee and strong brogue shoes. My mother was just the same as I remembered her, only browner. She wore a shabby cotton dress and open white sandals. Her blue eyes twinkled as she ran towards the bus. Clive waited in the background.

I hugged my mother. "It's so good to see you. I've so much to tell you. Did you get my letter from Capetown?" Without waiting for a reply I moved over to my father. I hesitated for a moment, not knowing whether to kiss him, hug him, or shake his hand.

He put his arm around me and said, "It's lovely to see you, my very own grown-up daughter." Those words meant a lot to me, for I could sense he was a silent undemonstrative man.

With my luggage stacked on and around the old Morris we set off for Pine Lodge. My father pointed out all the local landmarks, his office, the tea-shop, the Club and Government House. There were flowers everywhere, the bright red cannas lining the streets, mimosa and climbing orchids. The pine trees shed their needles across the road. When the tyres crunched over them there was a distinct scent. We turned into a long drive. "Welcome to Pine Lodge," said Clive proudly." I was disappointed with the first impression. The bungalow had a big verandah. The whole place was built of wood and raised on stilts. It seemed so fragile that a puff of wind would blow it over. Clive informed me that the stilts were to keep rats away. I shuddered. The car stopped at the front door. Four dark skinned men appeared, immaculate in long white shirts over baggy white trousers. They chorused, "Salaam, Missahib, salaam Missahib", putting their hands to their foreheads and bending forward. I smiled at them not knowing what else to do.

"What about a bath, Emma?" Ethel asked. "The sweeper brings the water and I heard him a few minutes ago."

"What a funny bath," I exclaimed when I saw the small zinc tub. It sat coldly on a concrete floor under a tap. "Does he do this all day?"

"That, and empty the lavatories. He's lower caste. Lives by himself at the end of the garden." Ethel turned the cold tap on slowly. "At least we've got cold running water." She turned to go. "Don't dawdle too much as it's already past time for tiffin."

That hot bath in the tin tub was the best I'd ever had. The lavatory was a bucket hidden discreetly in a wooden case with a hole in the top and the smell that came from the disinfectant made me realise I was in for a new lifestyle.

At my first family meal I explained about the excitements of the outward journey. Ethel prattled away, asking questions, but Clive remained silent though I could tell he was listening. Two servants waited at table. They were so quiet I hardly knew they were there.

Shillong

Clive took me to the bazaar and bought a bicycle for me and explained about the constant custom of bartering. He also told me never to touch a dog, never drink anything from a tap, and not to give things to begging children. There seemed much to learn. The news in Europe which we heard over our crackly wireless was grim with severe British losses on land. The blitz was taking a heavy toll. We felt guilty having all the comforts of peacetime and no blackout.

I wound bandages once a week for the Red Cross along with many other women whose husbands had come up from the plains to escape the torrid heat of the summer months. Ethel arranged for me to do a secretarial course. I

Emma at the age of 15

learned to play golf and better my tennis. There were a few other white girls in Shillong whose parents were permanently resident there. We were often called upon to the entertain the unattached young men who came to stay in the hills. My social life was restricted. I was only allowed out till 11 p.m on two nights a week. The other girls laughed at me.

When I became seventeen I began to feel that I should be doing more with my life than social engagements and playing tennis and golf. Clive found me a job in the Air Raid Precautions office. There was one white man in charge, a senior babu who smelt of beetlenut, and a young local Naga. No one knew what we were supposed to be doing, but the babu knew where to put his hand on me. I didn't like that.

"Funny place to be worrying about air raids," I laughed to Clive one evening. Shillong, high in the Naga hills of Assam, seemed remote from all worldly affairs, specially air raids."

"You never know, Emma. We aren't far from Burma," answered Clive cryptically. I felt he knew more than we did. As I knew there was a hundred miles of wooded mountain land between the two countries I put his words out of my mind, and continued to feel safe. Clive was a man of few words. Ethel was the one who talked, loved me and fussed over me. They didn't talk much to each other.

My calendar filled up with social engagements. I played golf after work. The brick built golf club was perched on top of a hill, overlooking what had been a polo ground and race track. The course was long, dry, with crafty ups and downs and well placed trees. James, an excellent golfer, came into my life. We played twice a week and he taught me a lot. Tall, ugly with a broken nose, he spoke in a quiet voice and he had a wonderful sense of humour. We danced together in the evening. There was no squeezing or pressing. We were good friends.

"You're so patient with me, James" I said one day when I had bunkered my second shot.

"Being patient is part of the job of A.D.C to the Governor," came the good humoured reply. "But it's a change from being a policeman. I'd done ten years of that."

"That makes you 29," I calculated. "I'm only 17. Why on earth do you bother with me?"

He took me home in his car, and as we drove slowly down our drive, he put his hand on my knee. "All right for Friday? As usual? You know I like being with you, don't you?" Through the pine trees the moon shone on his face and I saw his quizzical look. I felt excited and strangely disturbed.

That Friday after golf James, fresh from his shower and smelling of talcum powder, suggested that we should go for a drive. "I'd love to," I replied. I wore a new clean frock, my sweaty golf clothes were squashed untidily in my holdall. "The sun'll just be setting," said James and drove to a little knoll where we watched the small lights of the town flicker as the evening drew in. The pine trees darkened and pointed severely to the sky as the sun dipped. Wiffs of smoke rose from nearby huts tingling our nostrils with the smell of spices. We didn't speak much, there was no need. Then James put his arms around me and kissed me on my mouth, my first kiss. "I've wanted to do that for a long time," he said quietly. "You're very lovely, but I didn't want to frighten you. It's so refreshing to find someone who is innocent." I stayed quiet in his arms. When he put his palm over my breast I tensed up - danger signals. James sensed my unease and drove me home.

The war was raging in North Africa. London was being bombed every night but nothing changed in Assam. James and I saw each other for several weeks. We danced, walked in the pine trees, played golf and talked. We kissed and cuddled in his car on the way back from the Club in the moonlight, but that was as far as it went.

One night, some friends joined us for dinner at James' quarters. After the meal, I went to James's bedroom with the other ladies of the party to tidy myself. I looked around his room, all masculine with brown fittings. There on his dressing table, in a silver frame, was a photo of a beautiful girl. Her long blonde tresses curled over her shoulders. I stood staring at it. I couldn't believe that James had another girl and had never told me. I had trusted him completely. This girl was slim, stylishly dressed and she had an air of self-possession. I slapped powder on my nose and wobbled a lipstick round my lips. With my head held high and my mouth firmly shut to stop my lips from quivering, I returned to the party with the other girls.

Naga Tribesman

When the last guest had gone James turned to me. "Went alright don't you think?"

I couldn't answer. I couldn't control the tears.

"Why, Emma, what's the matter?"

"Why didn't you tell me?" I sobbed openly now, quite out of control.

14

"Ah, the photo." He led me to a chair and lent me his big handkerchief. "That photo... She's Ellen. She's Norwegian. We got engaged to be married in 1939. Now I can't even get in touch with her 'cos of this damn war. What should I do? I can't do more than tell you I love you. I can't ask you to marry me, much as I've wanted to."

The house in Shillong

He put his head into his hands. I heard his story out, and felt his pain. Events were out of our control.

In the early part of 1942 I still adored James and was thankful to have a steady boyfriend as escort to parties and as a golf partner. We heard of the dark and difficult conditions in the U.K and I thought of Aunt Mathilda and Di trying to live on their rations and coping in the blackout. Petrol and food, both scarce in England, were not restricted in Shillong. I was so absorbed in myself that I took no notice of the anti-British riots and propaganda rumbling away on the plains. Our servants were loyal though the pay they received and conditions they lived in were in great contrast to the white residents' standards. But they were rich compared with the rice-grower, tea pickers or city dwellers. These people lived in shanty towns with no running water or drains.

But change was to come as Clive had predicted. The events in Burma crescendoed to disaster. The Japanese had invaded from the south and east and the whole white population was being evacuated. Most were hounded towards the Assam/Burmese border, women and children, sick and old. They had to walk, scramble, cut their way through the jungle, trekking for miles across mud-sodden paths, negotiating the virgin forests and great heights as well as they could. Malaria and dysentery were rampant. Many died on the way. The British and Indian armies were sent up through Imphal, a town right on the border in the jungle. Their task was to halt the Japanese but they themselves had to retreat. Shillong, being the nearest big town to the Burma border, was soon receiving the exhausted and frightened families and the tired and often sick troops. The number of new arrivals swelled rapidly.

Many of us tried to help. Military units were assembled to hasten the urgent need for hospitals, homes and military quarters. The road up to Shillong and the longer road to Imphal up the Assam valley needed strengthening. Both

15

Emma as a captain of the WAC(I) aged 17

were being used by heavy military equipment. James was whisked away at very short notice to go to Imphal. He was the only man available who could speak the local dialects and they needed to recruit native people who knew how to work in the jungle. I felt bereft when he had gone but knew I was only one of many who were suffering separation.

I felt I had to do something more positive. I decided I would try to join up. I knew I would face opposition from Ethel, but I thought that Clive would support me. I applied to the Womens' Auxiliary Corps of India, or W.A.C.(I) as it became known. I lied about my age and said I was eighteen. Straight away and without any training I was given the rank of Captain. I became A.D.C to the local General, thereby releasing a younger officer for active service. No details of uniform were sent to me, so I had to make up my own design. I followed the men's wear as much as I could. I had a short straight skirt made as well as long trousers. The local derzhi came and sat on the verandah and used Ethel's ancient machine to make up the garments. While he was fitting the bush-jackets with square pockets on the bosom like the men, he took care to have a good fondle at my breasts. He was a dirty old man, with a goatee beard, but I said nothing. I had no square drill training and had no idea whom I should salute or what to do if someone saluted me. I usually took off my neat fore and aft cap and put it in my pocket to avoid formalities.

Shillong became more and more like a military cantonment. The small curving paths through the pine trees were widened and battalions of soldiers were housed in wooden huts hidden from an aerial view. The R.A.F were billeted on the far side of town in similar huts. Two new hospitals appeared in weeks and were quickly filled, the majority of patients were servicemen ill with malaria and severe dysentery caused by the jungle conditions.

Faithful servant

I worked in the Area Headquarters set up on the outskirts of Shillong. I had no idea how I was going to be involved. All I knew was that I was letting a young man off from an office job so that he could go on active service. The

General and his staff were to organise and prepare for the re-advance through the jungle back into Burma. Food supplies, engineering supplies, new runways, huts, hospitals, roads all had to be considered, sometimes reconnoitred and then budgeted for.

It soon became clear that the war in North Africa had the first priority for arms, men and munitions and that now there were not enough resources to meet the demands of a jungle war against the Japanese. Strong reinforcements were sent from the U.S.A together with their heavy engineering equipment and expert knowledge of road building and road maintenance in all conditions. Fighting soldiers also came from Africa, New Zealand and Australia.

The effect that the soldiers from the States had on the local economy was unnerving. With their huge pay packets they could out price any offers our soldiers made for the company of a girl, whether brown or white. This left our men with little to do. As a result many of them resorted to drinking the local beer. Even in the relaxed conditions of a hill station fights started between the two armed forces. The Americans outbid the set rate for domestic staff and most of the trained servants went to work for them. Fortunately after twenty five years of continuous employment our own servants were loyal to Clive and Ethel, but we gave them extra rice rations. This was a real bonus as rice was in short supply. The civil authorities were stock-piling it in case India was invaded and the fields couldn't be cultivated.

On the first day of work a large three-ton lorry creaked its way to Pine Lodge to pick me up. Its high square roof knocked down some of the trailing orchids, and the heavy tyres dug into our drive. When I opened the door to the main office in the Headquarters I saw all heads turn my way and I felt they were mentally undressing me. I was the only girl on the premises. All I could see were khaki uniforms. I hoped that I'd be accepted and be able to hold my own.

The officers stood up to shake my hand but I was not made to feel welcome. When I met the General I relaxed for under the shaggy eyebrows beamed friendly eyes, the grey hair and gentle manner made him seem more avuncular than a senior military officer. He was efficient and far-seeing and introduced me carefully to my new role. I was told that I was to accompany him when he was on tour in upper Assam. I had to make life straightforward for him, booking accommodation either with tea planters or in the dak bungalow, a dwelling reserved for travelling white people - horribly scruffy with the barest of cooking and sanitary facilities. No linen or food was provided; sometimes there was no electricity. I had to book train tickets and see the car was in order. He had to be free to concentrate on the matters in hand and I was to take note of all the orders and plans.

On return from the travels I was expected to put everything that had been decided down in writing. During the summer months of 1942 the General and his entourage, with me in tow, made long journeys of over five hundred miles in the hot, wild and sometimes unexplored country. We spent nights camped in the jungle, with mosquitos a constant annoyance. We commandeered a local vessel to view the banks from the river. We looked for suitable sites for aerodromes, water points, transit camps, gun sites, hospital sites, and advance dressing stations, in fact everything that an advancing military force would be likely to need. I was supposed to remember people's names and their units and write the necessary thank you letters when we had received hospitality.

At the beginning and end of each journey was the long and twisting road from the plains to Shillong. Once on the plains there was the one main road running north east, with a branch off it to Imphal and Kohima. This road was full of potholes, and it followed the slow moving but colossal Brahmaputra. The General eyed this river as a future source for moving military equipment, another thing for my list. The single road was unsuitable for heavy and fast traffic. The cattle sought sanctuary on the tarmac, it was cooler than the surrounding dried mud.

I had only a smattering of 'kitchen hindustani' but nobody seemed to bother. When I booked in at the dak bungalows I didn't know whether to reserve a room specially for myself for that meant that the senior officers had to double up. No one told me anything. I had to find out for myself. I had also to come to terms with very tricky lavatory problems. In a male world no arrangements were made for separate facilities for me. I had trouble in negotiating some of the manly shaped objects. It was far preferable to be given hospitality in a tea planter's house or with a local doctor. They often had wives, or mistresses, who were able to take me under their wing. The women also enjoyed a chat with a new female face, and plied me with questions about 'home' and what had gone on in their beloved England.

I tried hard to make the journeys run smoothly, but occasionally there were hiccups, which were not always my fault. The General and I were due to catch the only midday train up the line to see the opening of a new military hospital. The General, while consulting a field officer and drinking a whiskey, didn't appear to be conscious of the time. I kept looking at my watch and saw the hands creeping towards the time of departure. Much as I tried to draw his attention to the clock, he wouldn't budge.

"Sir," I announced in a firm voice when I felt we could delay no longer. "We've got that train to catch. We can't possibly afford to miss it. So much has been planned for your arrival."

At last he hurried himself, but as we arrived at the station we saw the only train draw out.

"Damnation" he said. "You go and see what the station master can fix." When he saw the hesitation on my face he said, "Hurry, woman, that's an order."

I knocked at the clerk's door and made wild gesticulations with my hands, saying quickly, quickly. The clerk called the station master. Fortunately he spoke a little English. To move two white officers and one Indian driver up the line when the only passenger train of the day had gone was a complex problem for him. He scratched his head. Then a smile spread across his face. He would put us on a goods train which was due in half an hour. I put this suggestion to the General and he grunted, so I gave the go ahead to the station master to stop the goods train so that we could get aboard. When the train chuffed into the station all the closed trucks were at the front, the open flats were at the rear. The station master fussed around and produced two wicker chairs and a stool and placed them on one of the empty open flats. The stool was for the driver. I eyed a large black cloud and heard the rustling over the trees, an ominous sound which heralded rain. At this very moment the station master came panting up with three large black umbrellas, one for the orderly on his stool and one for each of us. He promised to phone the expectant unit to say how and when we were arriving. We looked ridiculous and the General scowled. The Colonel who greeted us on our arrival, wet and dirty, kept a straight face as if this was the usual mode of travel for his senior officer.

On another of our long tours we stayed with some tea planters just outside Tezpur. "We're going to look for a new site for some guns," the General announced at breakfast. "There'll be quite a big party, five or six cars. Here's the mark on the map, and that's where we'll lead the convoy to. I'll drive and you sit beside me and direct me."

I felt totally confident, but my mind must have been distracted; there were so many new things to see, small temples, beautiful flowers and monkeys everywhere. Six cars were following behind, all filled with officers of differing ranks. We passed through a small town and then took a single track road, which went on and on. None of the landmarks seemed like anything on my map. I turned it round and round, hoping to pick up something familiar. The single track road we were on got smaller and smaller, and finally it petered out in a steep mud-banked gully leading to a fast stream. All the cars queued up behind.

"And what now?" was the only comment the General made. He got out of the car, walked a few yards away and started to pee. This seemed to give the signal to the other officers in the convoy, and soon a line of khaki shirted men stood with their backs to me all relieving themselves. I was dying to pee too, but in no way could I clamber up the steep bank. I had to walk all the way past the convoy to the end of the cutting and then find myself a small bush. When I returned the General had half a smile on his face. I think he saw the funny side of the situation. It took several hours for the vehicles to disengage themselves from the cul-de-sac for it became more and more churned up as each vehicle tried to reverse. I was not given any more map reading.

Six weeks later we did an extended journey to Digboi, a small town which was rich in oil. It was also near the road which led up to Imphal, Kohima and the Burma border. There was an American airfield already established close by with hutted accommodation around its perimeters. The General wanted to pick the brains of the American Officers about the local conditions and terrain. The American mess was in a huge marquee with straw mats laid over the floor. Proper tables with flowers, smart shiny cutlery and sparkling glasses made our own entertaining efforts near the front line look shoddy. Our party, the General, five officers and myself, were given a sumptuous meal.

Again I was the only girl and I was dying to relieve myself. When I asked a junior officer what I should do he pointed to a row of huts in the middle of a large field. As I walked across the field I felt I was causing a stir. Each hut had a wicker-like wobbly door. I opened the first door and was greeted by an astonished squatting brown man with a large pair of surprised eyes. I walked along the line of doors and opened several more to be greeted with the same surprise, then a chorus of catcalls. I went back to find the young officer. He managed to produce a tin bucket and plonked it in his tent. I didn't like to leave my offerings for the young officer to dispose of, so I watered the tent pegs and left quickly for the General's party.

He called over to me and explained that there was to be a flight over the drome and he asked if I would chose to go with them. I accepted quickly. The General, several high ranking American officials and the senior officers of our staff all piled into the plane. It was stripped of all fittings in its interior, and small crates were put along the sides and we all sat on those. I was fortunate to be given a crate up front, and the handsome pilot eyed me with approval as he came to give an account of the flight plans. He asked the General if he could show me the cockpit to see how things worked. The General agreed, his eyes twinkling. We zoomed over the trees. The pilot and I talked of this and that while he took his machine in swoops over the countryside. The tea gardens looking like crinkled velvet, were interrupted by small hair-like roads. The villages seemed like buttons spilt from a button box. The long main road lay like a sturdy white ribbon, the travelling military vehicles seemed stationery. The brooding dark jungle covered the hills and mountains. There was a sense of power in the throbbing engine. The pilot interrupted my thoughts.

"Well now. How about a special treat? Would you like to handle the joystick?" He gave me instructions about pushing it for going down, and pulling it for going up. He smiled all the time.

"Seems easy," I said with a grin, and pulled hard on the joystick. "Heavens, girl. Not that hard."

There was an urgent knocking on the intervening door. An irate officer demanded to know what had happened. "Must've got in an air pocket, sir," replied the young pilot, flashing signals to me with his eyes.

"Thank you for the cover-up," I said. The sudden swoop upwards had unseated all the military officials from their boxes and they had landed in an undignified heap on the floor of the plane.

After a few months I began to feel I was not pulling my weight though nobody had complained. I thought that a lone woman in a man's world caused difficulties with single accommodation and sanitary arrangements. Everyone had been polite to me, and I felt safe. I felt they had a code of honour not to swear in front of me. Nobody touched me up. Thanks to James I felt able to talk to people on even terms, but still I wondered if I was more trouble than I was worth. On one of the long journeys back to Shillong I began to think about my role and whether I should look for other work. But on my arrival home, a letter from G.H.Q Delhi changed everything and decided matters for me. It stated coldly that after a period of six months it was decided that the job of A.D.C was not suitable for a W.A.C.(I) owing to the stringent conditions so that I was to be relieved of my post. It also stated that as there were no other positions of officer status in the district, I would have to relinquish my commission. I was offered a job instead in the newly started Cipher Office in the Military Headquarters in Shillong and would hold the rank of private. I was to reply immediately if I wanted the post. The implications of losing my commission did not worry me as I had no real idea of the esteem of officer status, nor did the drop in salary concern me. But I hadn't realised that my colleagues thought I was a non-starter. They had all been so polite. I showed the letter to my parents the following morning. "I've only made a few mistakes," I said. "People seemed to think I was O.K. Why wasn't I consulted?" I kept my thoughts to myself about the difficulties with accommodation and sanitary arrangements.

"Can't do anything about it," replied Clive, filling his pipe. "Orders from the top are orders. I'm not sorry though. Having you galavanting round the countryside has been a worry for us."

"But you said, "well done," when I started."

"You're still so young, Emma. Can't think why we let you get involved. Motoring about the jungle with a lot of men. Quite out of your depth, I'd say." Clive got up from his chair and left the room suddenly.

"Oh Mum." I turned to Ethel. "Why doesn't he talk more to me about it? Have you a hand in this?" Ethel giggled nervously and fiddled with the teapot. "Come on, Emma. Shall I help you send a wire? You'll accept the cipher work, won't you? You don't need a Captains's pay while you're living at home. The ciphering should be very interesting with all the troops moving here and there." I felt anger creep up my throat and accepted the new offer.

G.H.Q responded quickly. I was to start in the cipher office as soon as possible with the rank of a private. I took the three pips off my shoulders, wore the same uniform, and presented myself at the local Headquarters, this time on

Emma as Lieutenant in 1942 aged 18

my bicycle to suit my more lowly status. There was no three-ton lorry. The ride took twenty minutes. It was all up hill. I was puffing as I approached the khaki camouflaged unit. The Head Clerk made me feel welcome and led me down long corridors with hastily fitted ply-wood walls on each side. He was a family man who had joined up for the war and took things as they came. He eyed me quizzically for he saw the holes that the captain's pips had made in my epaulette. We were six in the team, three on duty round the clock. We were allocated an area at the far end of the building where it was supposed to be quiet. The trouble was all the other five smoked, so I gazed at the figures through a blue haze. The cipher books were very large and heavy with pages and pages of numbers. Each group of four figures had to be moved around and taken away from another group of four figures and then a message appeared. I seemed to get the hang of it very quickly and the Head Clerk was pleased with me.

"You're as good as any one of us," he puffed, smoke pouring from his nose. "You can see everythin' 'appening all up the Assam Valley, all the plannin' for the new army. Mighty secret, this. Gotta keep yer mouff shut."

"Sure thing," I replied. I didn't tell the Head Clerk that I already knew where most of these new ventures were going to be put. No one knew what I had been doing. The Cipher Office work came to a sudden end with another letter from G.H.Q. Delhi. I was assigned to "Q" branch of the Headquarters. This dealt with the actual building of quarters, movement of troops and supplies, and generally submitting quotes.

"Look at this, Mum," I laughed. "I'm to be promoted to Lieutenant, put one pip back on my shoulder, and carry on wearing the same uniform." During the winter months, and while I was in "Q" branch we had to take advantage of the weather. The days in Shillong were fine and dry, with blue skies and crisp air, perfect for convalescence. In the plains it had been the ideal time to do as much building and construction work as possible and take reinforcements up to the Burmese border. The work in my Headquarters piled up and my days were full; everyone worked long hours. The work done by the American forces was invaluable. Many of them came to Shillong from the plains for recuperation. I realised that everything about them showed a different life-style. Everything seemed big, their cars, huge army trucks and big voices. I watched sadly as they colonised the town, making life difficult for our own soldiers. Shillong became busier and busier. The hospitals were growing rapidly to deal with the troops sick with malaria and dysentery. The military headquarters expanded to cope with planning strategy for the oncoming attack back through Imphal and up and over the mountains. The soldiers and airmen who were physically well but training hard needed entertaining in the evenings as there were no pubs and only one tiny cinema. All the girls were asked to go dancing with them, and military vehicles did a round picking everyone up. We danced continuously till midnight when the band stopped and we were trucked back home again. Many of the troops wore their army boots and our feet got crushed, but fortunately several were beautiful dancers. Most of the men were homesick and between dances we were shown grubby photos of wives, sweethearts and children. I was exhilarated, but after a long day's work terribly tired, emotionally and physically. One ordinary Sunday during the ritual of going to evensong something happened that changed my life.

Part Two
Powerful love

There he was, sitting in the front row of the church next to the General. I slid into the pew behind. This tall blond officer with his arm in a sling kept flashing me glances as he turned to pick up his books. He looked gorgeous with his tidy tunic and tartan trousers. I could see a smile behind his thick moustache. I had a kind of hollow feeling in my stomach. The church service continued in a haze. After the service a group of people gathered in the church porch. I tried to squeeze through but I heard a voice call "Emma". It was the General for whom I had done some office work the previous morning. I walked up to him slowly for I realised that the handsome officer was by his side.

"I just want to thank you for your extra help yesterday," he said. "Now I don't expect you've met Peter, Major White. Peter, this is Emma, but damn it, I've forgotten your other name."

"Emma Robson," I replied shyly and after a pause I added, "Sir". That never came naturally to me. I turned to Peter, my heart thumping loudly.

"Hello, Emma." Peter was at ease immediately. He saw me glance at his arm. "That's not as bad as it looks," and he laughed. "Damned boil went sceptic in the heat. It's difficult to keep

Major Peter White

cool and clean under canvas. Look here, I don't know anyone yet. P'raps we could meet..." Out of the corner of his eye he saw the General walking to his waiting staff car. "Sorry, I must fly."

He turned briskly and reached the car in time to open the door. I walked the short distance to the Club wondering how I could negotiate another meeting with this handsome man. As I arrived at the carpark I saw the staff car stop at the Club entrance. Peter stepped out briskly, saluted and walked through the

main door. I followed him into the foyer and saw him turn into the library. I walked quietly in after him and knocked some books off a table, accidentally on purpose.

Peter appeared smiling. "Let me help," he said. "Did they conveniently fall?", and he let out a hoot of laughter. The clerk hissed for silence. We replaced the books and looked at each other. "This calls for a drink," he said. The drink was quickly followed by dinner. I felt quite free to talk about anything and everything. Peter was just as uninhibited. He walked me home, taking my hand, then my arm. My stomach turned over when he touched me. We walked across the wooden bridge over the lake where I had shed tears for James. This time I had tears of joy on my cheeks for I was with a man who I instantly recognised was the one person I wanted to be with forever. Peter, concerned that he had upset me, tried to kiss the tears away. As the drive to Pine Lodge drew nearer Peter became business-like.

"Emma, I've got three days before I have to go on an Intelligence course the other side of India. The medics think my arm will be better by then. If they say so, I have to go, specially now that things are hotting up round here. We must meet again and again before then. Can you manage that?" He looked at me anxiously. I nodded. "And," he continued, " I want to meet your parents. I want them to see that I'm not a baby snatcher. I'm twenty-seven, you know, been around a bit."

"I can get to the Club tomorrow at six o'clock after work," I whispered. "We'll walk back here, and then you can meet my parents."

Peter kissed me again very gently. I was too full up for words so I turned and climbed up the steps on to the verandah, stepping over Dhil Mahommad who slept curled up on his mat. I stood by my window watching the moon dip behind the hill. My thoughts were a riot. I knew I had fallen in love at first sight despite what people said. I had never dreamed of emotions like this. I watched the moonbeams shine like dancing fingers across the valley before I crept into bed, eager for events to unfold. At breakfast I told Clive and Ethel that I had met a Major Peter White and that I'd like to bring him for a drink to meet them and then go out together afterwards that evening. "That's fine," Ethel replied, "come about seven, and I'll tell cook you won't be in for dinner." Clive gave me a quizzical look but said nothing. At exactly 5.30 I tidied my desk, left a few unimportant files in the 'in' tray and cycled to the Club. I brushed my hair and straightened my clothes. I felt nervous, sort of hollow with excitement.

Peter was waiting under the trees. "I'm so glad you've come. The bottom would've fallen out of my boat if you hadn't taken me seriously. Come, let's sit in the shade." The moments flew by as we talked. The time for Peter to be vetted by my parents came round too fast. We walked briskly along the winding road, hand in hand, with Peter wheeling my bike. He was comfortable now with his arm out of a sling.

"Don't let's stay too long," I said.

"They've got to look me over," Peter giggled. "Feel a bit like a horse being vetted."

"I'm sure they'll like you," I reassured him. Actually I knew he would be acceptable because of his gentlemanly background. He was just the kind of man my parents liked, son of a Scottish gentleman, public school, Sandhurst, commissioned into a crack regiment and of course clean finger nails. We stayed for an hour and Peter withstood their critical glances. I felt proud of him. As soon as it was diplomatic we left and walked back to the Club.

"I wonder if my parents will give you such a looking over," Peter said with a smile. Realising that Peter was thinking of the far away future made me light-headed. We came again to the little wooden bridge across the lake. Peter stopped, and turned me round to look at him, his face serious.

"You know, Emma," he said firmly taking my hands in his. "You know, don't you, that I want you to marry me." I gasped, blood pounded in my head. Peter repeated himself. "Emma, I want you to marry me. Have you heard?"

"Yes, I've heard you. I'm a bit shaken up that's all." I knew I must play for time. My mind went round and round. I knew Peter was the only man for me, but, but, but.. "Oh, Peter," I said in a whisper. "Can't you see that you've knocked me sideways. Can't you tell I need you. But I feel so helpless and inexperienced that I..."

"Come on, old girl, we've only got three days. What's the point of waiting. Let's get married before I go. I'll get the C.O to fix it. I've never been so sure of anything in my life."

"Peter, you're going too fast. You're frightening me. Of course I want to marry you, but it's too much all of a sudden." I shook all over, even my teeth chattered.

"Oh, precious, I'm sorry. I've rushed my fences again." He took me in his arms and held me tight. "Come on, darling, let's go and have our meal. We'll find a quiet table, and I promise to try not to frighten you any more. Half of me can understand, but I need..." He left the sentence unfinished. He turned me round and we walked up to the Club without further words.

Tucked away in a corner of the large room, with the waiters silently tending to our needs Peter put his cards on the table. "I'm so much older than you, pet, mucked around a bit. Had sex with plenty of girls and you seem so untouched." He saw me colouring. "Why, Emma, you're embarrassed. There's no need to be. I can show you everything, just as you want it. But you must try to trust me. Try to think it's right for us to be together. Try to..."

"Don't go on, Peter," I beseeched. "Know that I adore you, but give me more time. Wait for me, wait..."

"Of course I'll wait," Peter interrupted. "But I NEED you now. You can grow up as my wife. With this damn war you never know what may happen. Casualties everywhere in Europe and now they're starting in Burma. You just can't tell. I'm a regular soldier, so I must fight and fight where ever I can."

The enormity of what Peter was saying crushed me. Two of my girl friends had lost their sweethearts in the last month. Suddenly I realised it could happen to me. I started to cry again, cursing myself as I did so.

"Come on, precious. We were supposed to be having a happy evening. And now I've made you sad again."

I tried to smile. Peter continued, "When this month's course is up, I'll be coming back here to train with my unit. I don't think they are ready for the front just yet. We'll have time to be together and talk about our future."

I felt safer when Peter deviated from the subject of immediate marriage. "I'll never forget anything you've said," I whispered. "And I'll wait for you feeling I already belong to you. But let's keep this a secret. I don't even want to tell Ethel just yet."

Peter became serious. "I applied to go on this Intelligence Course as I thought it'd help me to be in the nub of things and also perhaps when I retired from the Army."

"But that's miles ahead," I said. I shuddered at the dangers lurking in the future. After a pause I added slowly, "All I know now is that I just want to be with you and dissolve myself in your love."

"My silly, darling girl," he laughed, and kissed me on the forehead.

The next evening Peter waited for me again at the Club. We decided to buy sandwiches from the bar and walk across the hills to watch the lights come on over the little town. It was an hour's walk through the pine covered alleyways, the dry needles smelling medicinal as we crushed them. An occasional squawk came from a sleepy bird. At last we climbed a small hill, bare of all trees and before us stretched Shillong. In the sunset the bowl of the valley glowed rose-tinted, lights flickered in the small far away huts. Nearer, the hospitals, Government House and the European houses and military cantonments blazed with electricity, all windows uncurtained.

"What more could I want?" I asked. "I've the evening ahead, and I'm walking alone with my tall and handsome man. I'm talking from my heart, and I'm loving being loved." Peter was silent, but he squeezed my hand. We found a curved stone which faced the valley and here we rested. In the quietness my mind went beserk. The bumpy roads, the unfinished buildings in the jungle, the hospitals whose beds were already full, a real smell of dettol washed over me as I pictured bound stumps of arms and legs, and lavatories overflowing with excreta. All the horrors that were around, but not spoken about. I wished these thoughts would go away so that I could stay in the beauty of the moment with Peter on the hilltop. I shivered and Peter took me gently and sat me between his legs so that I could feel the warmth of his body.

"Emma, darling. I'm going to give you a little sermon. Don't laugh at me. But I must say these things just in case there's no time again. You never know." He paused and I felt the icy hand of fate down my back. "I've great plans for the future, after the war. I have a need to help people in trouble, and perhaps if I can do well on the battle field people will respect me more and listen to me." I stayed silent.

"Go on, Em, say something. Don't just sit here staring."

"You'd be wonderful at anything you do. But I'd be hopeless. I'm such a duffer at everything, except sport, and what good would that be..?"

"Stop running yourself down, girl. That's one thing I'm going to teach you. To think good of yourself. Look how well you've got on in the W.A.C.(I)." Silence again, broken only by the chirp of the crickets. "Let's plan for what we can do together." Instead he took me in his arms and kissed me.

Sitting so close between his legs I felt him harden. I knew what was happening after my cuddles with James in the car. "You know what you're doing to me, don't you, precious?" I nodded and smiled. "Well, I'm not going to let it go any further," Peter said with emphasis. "Up here, miles away from anyone it could all be so easy, but I'm determined to hold myself in check. It's not my strong point, but I'll try."

I nodded sagely, not really understanding what he was getting determined about. "Come now," he urged having glanced at his watch. There's just enough light from the moon to help us on our way down. I'm going to give you one last kiss that will have to last for a month, but remember, you are mine, today, tomorrow and for ever."

"Too right, I'll remember. But try to be careful. If anything happened to you, I would live the rest of my life only half alive. To meet you, love you, and have to part so soon is cruel. Damn the war, damn, damn." I kicked at a stone, frustrated at the thought of Peter's departure. My life seemed in turmoil with his arrival and my new wonderful love of him and the pressures of work in "Q" branch. Too much was happening too quickly. The Generals, whose troops were actually on the ragged front line, demanded more support, more supplies, the administrators for the support materials demanded more equipment, and the sick and wounded needed more attention. The little railway up the Assam Valley was not big enough for the demand and the supplies were not forthcoming. "Q" branch had to respond to the difficulties as well as they could. The war in Europe had to have top priority and the Fourteenth Army, waiting to pounce back into Burma was still at the bottom of the War Office list for weapons, medical supplies and basic English tinned food.

The support from the Americans was invaluable and their Air Force was co-opted to help with the parachute-dropping to the forward lines. The Burmese border was a difficult to defend. Wet sticky mud prevented the quick passage of men and materials. Malaria was the hidden enemy, together with typhus and dysentery. Poor living conditions and the heat allowed these diseases to multiply.

The month with Peter on his course went by fast. Letters to him took a week each way, and telephone calls were crackly.

On his return to Shillong he worked in Divisional Headquarters in the Intelligence branch. He was no longer in command of a company of his beloved regiment. We met whenever and where ever we could, talking, loving and planning. They were golden moments for time together was at a premium. The shadow of separation and thoughts of the dangers of war lay unspoken between us. It was hard to mix romance with duty.

One weekend when we walked alone through the woods with a free half-day ahead of us I asked a question which had been puzzling me. "Wouldn't you rather be with your men, Peter, with your own battalion? I always thought they were your top priority. Now you're stuck at a desk job." "Really and truly, I would," Peter replied seriously. "But it's back to the old maxim again. I must do what I think best to get closest to the enemy. You see, Em, this Burma war has been niggling on for nearly three years, and I've only had one direct contact with the Jap. That was when we were on the retreat. I managed to get my men out of danger, but that's not the same as fighting for victory. My whole life has been geared to leadership, and I think getting into Intelligence is as good a way of getting up that ladder." He put his arm round my shoulder. "I'm feeling a little impatient sitting up here in glorious Shillong, when things are hotting up in Europe. I'm sure we'll have to finish that campaign before we can really get going out here."

I started to feel uncomfortable. "Don't you like being in Shillong now that we've time to be together?"

"Don't take on so, Em," Peter sensed my nervousness. "Specially now, as I've something to tell you."

I felt sick with anxiety, the peaceful afternoon turning into a nightmare. Peter continued looking deep into my eyes. "About six months ago a letter came round asking for volunteers to return to the U.K to be trained for special services. I can't tell you what it is but the Intelligence course will be of some help."

"What are you saying, Peter? Are you...?" My voice trailed off.

"What I'm saying, Em darling, is that I put in then for repatriation to the U.K and volunteered for these special services." My breathing rasped in my chest and I had a tight pain across my forehead. "Perhaps I can fight the big battle in Europe and then come back here and help them clear up. I'm sure this campaign will be long and dreary and the one in Europe quicker." With a mixture of anger and despair I said in a low tone.

"And where do I come in?" Peter didn't answer my question.

"Do you think I'm mad, Em? Some of my fellow officers do. But try to understand me, precious, try to come to terms with the demon that drives me."

"S'ppose you must be right," I mumbled feeling it to be far from the truth.

Peter's voice broke into my thoughts. "Come on, old girl. Cheer up. You look as if I'd told you something awful, instead of something exciting. This is one of the reasons why I wanted you to marry me, quickly, now. Then you could travel as my wife. In war time conventions must be swept aside, things are so uncertain." He watched my face knowing that talk of immediate marriage made me uneasy. "There's been no call-up papers yet for my return, but the General knows all about it."

Silently we turned to retrace our steps. I felt a leaden lump in my chest. Few words passed between us on our return to Pine Lodge. He kissed me tenderly and lovingly with an anxious look in his eyes. That night I stood again at my bedroom window. The trees, sentinels in their different shapes, and the little stream became a backdrop to my turmoiled thoughts. A cloud of foreboding pressed down on me. Much as I love you, Peter darling, I can't bear what you are doing to me. Don't go, don't leave me. Please God, whoever and where ever you are, let some force look after Peter's soul and my soul and let us remain entwined together. I just can't bear the thought of him leaving for England. I was emotionally exhausted and lay down on my cool sheets hoping for sleep. I closed my eyes but my thoughts roamed. In the morning my limbs were heavy and my head throbbed.

The bridge

One evening three weeks later we planned to meet again after work on the wooden bridge. As I walked along the familiar road I saw Peter was already waiting. Restlessly, he picked up twigs and tossed them into the water. He looked distracted, and his greeting was restrained.

"What is it, Peter? Has something happened?" I asked.

"Yes, it's come, and now it's here I am not sure that I want it. I've never been indecisive like this before, and Em, it's your fault." Peter looked angrily at me.

"What HAVE I done? What's my fault?" I clutched his arm.

"I've got my orders to return to the U.K immediately. There's a passage booked for next Saturday. It means I must leave on Monday." Silence, silence. "Say something, Emma. Don't just stand there."

Peter lost his self-control; I, for once, was in command. "You've got what you wanted, Peter. I s'ppose I should be glad, but I'm NOT." I stamped my foot and the little bridge shook. "I almost hate you for doing this." I realised quickly the horror of what I had said and rushed into his arms. "No, I don't Peter. No, really, I don't. You are my world, and now my world is being taken away."

His voice pierced my agitation. "It needn't be taken away, Em. We could go together. I could get a licence pre-arranged in Bombay, and you can travel as my wife. You can't get a passage nowadays unless you are married. Did you know that?"

"I can't marry you yet, Peter. I don't know enough about anything. Anyhow I'm doing my war work out here, and I think I'm doing a jolly good job. And..." Words came tumbling out. "And.. I've fallen in love with you so quickly; how do I know I won't fall in love with somebody else?"

"God forbid, Emma. You don't really think that," Peter interrupted.

"No, I don't think it now, but I don't KNOW. Damnit, you've got me all muddled up."

Peter became rational. "I know you're a minor, so first we've got to ask your parents' permission. Come, let's go. Into the lion's den?" He laughed uncertainly. We were both silent till we reached the familiar verandah steps. My thoughts whizzed round. I would leave home and security for what? To be with Peter as long as he was in England, but then where and how? Dil Mahommad greeted us and offered us drinks. Clive and Ethel appeared when they heard our voices. "Come and sit down," Ethel said. "Will you stay for supper?" I sat on the edge of my chair, Peter stood by the mantelpiece.

"No supper, thanks," I murmured. "Peter's got something to say." Peter turned to Clive who was peacefully filling his pipe. "It's like this, sir." He cleared his throat. I could sense his unease. "I've been posted back to the U.K. I've known it may happen, but the orders have just arrived. It's come as a shock, just when Emma has come into my life."

"Sounds exciting, wish I could get back," muttered Clive not sensing the tension.

"I've got to leave on Monday." Peter took no notice of the interruption. "That gives me three days." He paused and looked at the puzzled faces of the older people. Then the words came with a rush. "I want to marry your daughter and take her back with me as my wife."

Ethel drew in her breath and fluttered her handkerchief. Clive looked at Peter and asked in his most withering way, "And what do you propose to do with her when you get back to England? What can you offer her if you are sent to Germany? I presume that is where you want to end up?"

Peter, surprised by Clive's clinical and biting tone, defended himself as well as he could. His reasoning seemed fragile.

Ethel interrupted, her voice high with anxiety. "Peter dear. Emma is too young and inexperienced. I suggest that she waits a year and if she feels the same then, I promise we'll do our best to get you both together. I hope you agree with me, Clive."

Clive gave a sigh of relief not to have to make a decision and nodded. Peter looked exhausted and defeated. As soon as possible we left Pine Lodge and walked, walked just anywhere, bemused and unhappy. Angrily Peter said, "You didn't do much to help me. Can't understand your reasoning. Marry me, and we'd be together for as long as possible. Not marry me and time, oceans, years, war and a hundred other things will keep us apart."

"Kiss me, Peter. Hold me tight. Don't be so angry. I can't oppose my parents. Never have. But I promise I'll come to you."

Sadly and quietly we walked arm in arm amongst the pine trees. We didn't feel like eating, even talking was difficult. It was a tense week end. We met at the Club for lunch. Peter had spent the morning saying goodbye to his fellow officers and the troops of his old company. We talked and walked or just sat amongst the pine needles and watched the changes of the sky. Kissing and hugging were no longer important. The future, too ominous to contemplate, made our pain intense.

That Sunday night, with our meal still left on our plates and the wine untasted Peter said, "I'm going to take you back to Pine Lodge now. This tension is just too much."

Once more we walked over the little bridge, again the moon cared for our journey. At the verandah steps Peter stopped and whispered, "Write to me about everything, Em, good and bad. Forgive me for what I'm doing. I pray to God it's right. I'll wait for you always, but come as soon as you can."

My throat was too tight for words to come out. Peter took off his cap, bent over me and kissed me, the tears glinting in his eyes. All passion drained away. Without looking back I slowly walked up the steps. I wept myself to sleep that night. Even the moon went behind the clouds and all was dark. March 1943 crept by. I was determined to be cheerful and determined no one should know the burden of sorrow that the separation meant to me. Mail was slow and erratic. Only occasional loving letters arrived from Peter telling me of his journey and his time in England. In every letter he asked if I was ready for my own return home. I felt fraught and suffered increasingly bad headaches. One evening I came home early from work, cold and shivery. Ethel was out. Clive, holding his evening whisky and soda, came and sat with me. "I'm feeling awful, Dad," I muttered.

"You've been looking peaky these last weeks," Clive said. "Been watching you. You miss that Peter badly, don't you? Wish I could help more, but I feel so useless. Your mother is in control in this family. I'm so sorry..." "Don't say that," I interrupted. "You're a silent kind of pillar." Embarrassed that Clive should talk to me about his private life I continued, "You'll be the first to know definite news of Peter. But it's all so secret." I started to shiver violently and got up to go to bed.

"You just let me know when the time is ripe for you to join him, and I'll do all I can to get a passage." I turned to say good night, my teeth chattering.

"Hope it's not that damned malaria," Clive reached for my hand and squeezed it. It was a comfort to know that he understood.

As the April sunshine shone brightly into my bedroom I realised next morning I was really ill. I shivered uncontrollably, and my head seemed as if it was filled with walnuts knocking together. I called Ethel who called the doctor. He diagnosed malaria, and told me I must have been bitten when on tour up the Assam Valley. I felt I was now in the same plight as many of the serving soldiers who had recently arrived and I was glad to be in a comfortable bed with kind people to look after me, very different from the conditions in the jungle. For a week the fever took over, I shivered one moment, then sweated the next. No preventative medicine had yet been discovered; the only antidote to stop the current attack was neat quinine, larger and larger doses of foul tasting stuff. I lay on my bed, too hot to have the thinnest cover over me. My sheets became soaked in sweat and Dil Mahommad made sure I had clean ones twice a day. The sweeper brought constant warm water for I needed to wash frequently. Cook sent lemon and rice water, cool but not cold. The table boy brought flowers from the garden. Ethel was distraught. The doctor confirmed that the attack was a bad one and that more attacks would follow. My longing for Peter increased as I lay in bed. The worst part was not knowing where he was or what he was doing. War news from the Western front was gloomy. Bombing in England was sporadic. My morale was very low. When I had stopped shaking and sweating I wrote letters to Di and Aunt Matilda explaining about Peter and how I longed to get back to England. Soon a bunch of letters arrived from Peter. The words were written on an airagraph form, a sort of photographic condensed form of the original letter. It was open for any one to read which made writing about personal relationships inhibited. It was difficult to know exactly where he was as the only address allowed was a Field Post Office. I gathered that his parents had settled in Scotland and that he was not far away from them. He had also received my short letters again addressed to the Field Post Office. I longed for some communication which told me of his feelings. Soon my wish was granted. One evening after work I went to my room to change. Dil Mahommad knocked at the door, and smiling broadly he presented me with a fat envelope. I drew a chair to the window. Peter's writing was wiggly, so I could only read slowly. Dated June 1943 it read.

My darling girl, I'm sitting in a hotel bedroom, bathed and clean, and there is a whole hour before dinner. I'm going to try to make up for the short notes that I've written till now. I'm going to tell you everything, but please don't worry about some bits. First of all, thank you for your many letters. I worry about your malaria and losing all that weight. Do take care. Yes, time in passing, but not fast enough for me. I feel being apart so unnecessarily is waste, waste, WASTE. I'm sure, best beloved, we could manage somehow. Fortunately we are all so exhausted at the end of the day, all we can do is sleep. We have been out on endless exercises in all weathers trying to toughen us all up. My men have been wonderful and all back me up. You will see I am with the battalion again. I am not allowed to tell you more, but we are waiting for the time when we can put our training into effect. We have all been given a week's leave for working so hard. No parties, no sport, no girls. Now a bunch of us have come to London and we are making whoopee. I think you are too inno-cent to guess what we will try and do on this last night. But I'll take care. My parents have returned from Cairo and settled near Aberdeen. I've been able to see them - lovely after ten long years. Father is twenty stone now. I worry for his health. I hope you'll like him. Mother is fragile and may frighten you, but she's alright inside. Just a bit daunting from her immaculate appearance. They often visit London as Father still has business commitments. I'm still no-where near a battle and am getting a bit impatient if we stay up north much longer. There's so much going on in Italy as we know from the papers. Bombing is slackening off a bit. The queues for food are ghastly. Be prepared for that. Luckily eating in a Mess we don't have those problems and we seem to have plenty of everything. Father ate all his marmalade ration for a month at one breakfast. He'd no idea of rationing either after living in Cairo. I've been saving up for this London spree, as well as putting some money away for our BIG day. When that will be is up to you, but I'm waiting and missing you terribly. Fancy a grown-up man who's been around most of the world being so upset by just one girl. You are VERY special. I love you so much. Peter. (Writing to you makes me sad.)

Next day after work I went to my bedroom. I sat peacefully at my small table and started to write.

My darling Peter, Your long letter took a month. Reading it brought your presence closer. Thank you for writing about everything. I think I can guess what you all did on your last night. I'll pretend I don't mind. I can't pretend though that I understand why you are getting impatient if you stay up north. Why must you always be wanting to move to bigger things? Why do you have to do things in such a hurry? I thought you were with a crack Division of the highest calibre and yet you want to move on. Perhaps it's not ordained for you to be a hero and you will have to be a hero by example not deed. You are a hero to me whatever you do. Your parents sound a bit daunting and I've never been inside a London hotel so won't know how to behave. But I'll do my best not to disappoint you. Now I must tell you about my headaches. Really terrible they are. About once a fortnight, and I can hardly stand up. I'm sure it's all the tension of the moment, the indecisions. I've not told the doctor about you, so he can't really cure me, he just gives me stronger and stronger pills. I hope they will pass or at least get less severe. There's not much change in the pace of life here. Lots and lots of Americans, and they've taken over the golf course. That's now covered with large camouflaged tents. The road past Pine Lodge is spoilt with many huge trucks winding down it. Quite dangerous for me on my bike. Oh yes, I was coming home late from work in the dark and an Indian stepped out right in front of me, and tried to grab my bike. I just pedalled harder and knocked him over. Brave me. Ethel asked me why I was pink, but I just laughed and said I'd hurried. She'd start to fluster if I told her all the truth. Can't say I'm happy, 'cos I'm not, yet I manage to enjoy things. Nothing seems excruciatingly beautiful like it was when I was with you. Even the moonbeams aren't my friends. Darling, I love you, but the pain is terrible. Emmy.

The summer months ground by. One night in early September I had a terrible headache. It was so bad and my face was so pale that it aroused comments in the office and I was dispatched home early. Dil Mahommad was there to greet me, salver in hand, a letter from England on the salver. "Letter from Master Sahib," he said. Then he saw my face. "Miss Sahib not well. I get Miss Sahib hot drink?"

"Thank you, Dil Mahommad. Hot drink very nice. Head very bad. Yes, long letter from Master Sahib". I gave him a watery smile. When the hot drink arrived I took two aspirin, then sat by the bedroom window and opened the letter, slowly and with great anticipation. It was written in August and had taken 3 weeks to arrive. I read it carefully.

Emma, my precious. This is one of the most important letters I've ever written. I just can't wait for you any longer. We've been apart for six months now. Surely you know your own mind? Come to me, and we can have a little time together before I go. Be brave, my love. Stick up for yourself in front of your parents. Whatever you say, I'm going to announce our engagement in the papers then you will publicly belong to me. This might help you to get a passage back here. I'm sure there'll be many difficulties on that score. Another thing, darling. Don't think you are indispensable in your work. Any young officer who is battle weary and has to work away from active service could do your job, so could any older officer. Your job is with me, as my wife. Far more suitable for a woman, than careering around in uniform. Well now, what about it? My feelings for you are the same, even stronger. I even have imaginings of a small Peter around when I come back from overseas, but I suppose that's jumping the gun a bit. Try and accept this challenge. Try and jump Beecher's Brook just for once. You've always played safe in your life. Don't disappoint me this time. If you loved me as much as I love you there'd be no hesitation on your part. I'm waiting for you. With my love, your adoring Peter. P.S I won't write about local news in this letter. What I've said is too important.

I put the letter on my lap and looked out of the window. My breathing quickened. I knew I must accept and face up to Peter's challenge. Beecher's Brook was the most testing jump and it needed guts to have a go at it. What an ultimatum! Then I realised with a flash of disappointment how little value Peter gave to my work, when I thought I was doing such a splendid job. Never

35

mind that now, I reasoned. It's Beecher's Brook for me. With the letter in my hand I approached Clive and Ethel who were sitting on the verandah having a cup of tea. Ethel looked up expectantly, Clive drank from his large mug. "I've had a letter from Peter." I felt it was right to come to the point quickly. I sat on the edge of the chair and watched their puzzled eyes. "Now listen carefully. Peter has announced our engagement in the English national papers and he urges me to return to him." I paused. Ethel sighed and sat up straight. Clive put his mug down. "He says that after six months I should know my own mind and be able to act on my own decisions." I waited again, feeling that they were building up ammunition against my case. "Please, please don't oppose me any more. I stayed behind last time when you told me to. Now I'm older and stronger and I KNOW it's right for me to go."

"But Emma.." Ethel drummed her fingers on the chair arm.

"Please, please don't make it difficult. I'm really going to go, and I'd much rather it be with your blessings than have a row. Can't you understand, Daddy?" I appealed to Clive knowing that he had felt the sadness that I was holding.

He nodded twice.

Then I turned to Ethel. "Now, Mum, I know you are going to put up all sorts of obstacles. But I'll overcome them. Try stopping me and I'll show you." I felt the tone of my voice grate as my agitation increased.

Ethel flushed and grew angry. Clive replied to my direct appeal and I loved him for it. "I think you should give it a go, Emma. You've got guts, and I'm sure you'll manage. It's just that I don't like to think of you on your own in England. But you'll manage, you'll manage."

I was so overjoyed to hear his approval that I gave him a hug and a tear squeezed out of his eye.

"Come on, child, don't take on so." Clive was embarrassed and unused to affectionate demonstrations.

"What've you let her in for?" Ethel asked Clive aggressively. I felt she played delaying tactics. "She's got this good job, and a roof, and she's safe. How can you blithely say you think it's fine that she goes on her own to England? The war's on, the seas aren't safe. Remember the journey she had out here?" She stood up and paced along the verandah.

I felt hard-hearted as I said in a jubilant voice, "Sorry, Mum. It seems as if it's two against one and counting Peter, that's three. I'll miss this home and all you've both done for me, but I do feel able to cope now with whatever comes. Let me go with your love, Mum. Come on, give me a hug."

Ethel pulled herself together and came towards me and we both hugged. Then she laughed. "Don't you ever say I can't lose gracefully."

From that moment I had her support and straightaway we sat down, heads together, and started to make practical plans. Clive sighed with relief, grateful that Ethel had supported him. He pulled harder on his pipe and went back to his book. The first action I took was to send a telegram to Peter. It was addressed to the F.P.O address. It said, "Jumping Beechers stop Returning soonest possible stop Advise destination stop love you Emma.

After three weeks the reply from Peter arrived. "Well done stop life will be complete stop very proud stop writing instructions stop all adoration stop Peter.

Once the engagement was announced publicly congratulations poured in. When I gave notice in the office all my colleagues were happy. Ethel tried to be brave and Clive helped all he could. The plans to leave Shillong went very smoothly, but the hassle began when I tried to get a berth back to the U.K. Passages were only available to the armed forces and their relatives. I was not yet a wife and had to resign my commission on leaving India so I felt I would never qualify for a passage. Clive tried through civilian sources and Ethel tried through military channels but to no avail. Peter began to despair. When I was not working I spent the time trying to collect clothes suitable for an English climate and smart enough to wear in London. It was impossible. Only shoddy cotton goods were available. Fortunately in early December 1943 the Head Clerk came to me one morning with a circulation in his hand which he had just received. It explained that senior officers, brigadiers and above, were entitled to have a nanny travel with them, free of cost, on their return journey to the U.K. The Head Clerk wired G.H.Q and put my name up for a vacancy.

I sent a wire to Peter. It read, "Hopefully returning soonest passage available as Nanny stop excited stop Emma.

For once Peter's reply came within the week. The excitement brought warmth and urgency into my plans.

Christmas passed in a daze, my heart was not in all the social activities that we were asked to do. The drastic battles starting up on the Burma front made no impression on me. It was only when I saw the wounded and very ill in the hospitals that the reality of war struck me. I visited the soldiers, I talked to them, I wrote letters for them, but my mind was not with them or their problems. I craved for my big love at the end of my journey. Everyone was surprised when a telegram from G.H.Q detailed me to report to Bombay on 7th February 1944 to be a nanny to Brigadier Henderson and his family on their return journey to the U.K. In two weeks I had to start the long train journey across India. The days were hectic. Ethel wept, the servants were silently extra attentive. Nobody spoke of the danger or the bombing, or the invasion of Europe that was bound to come. Clive was staunch in his support and arranged for friends to meet me both at Calcutta and Bombay. A final telegram was sent to Peter. It read, Nanny leaving Shillong second February stop sailing fastest possible stop love Emma.

I had managed to collect a few possessions that I thought might help to start a home. I had several pieces of local wood carvings, some coarse cotton sheets, a coffee set and a few local rugs. Even these humble pieces filled several cases. The clothes I needed were in a separate trunk. All my luggage, save for a small case for the long journey were booked through to Bombay. Clive and Ethel drove me down the steep hill to catch the train for Calcutta. As I left the house for the last time all the servants stood in a row and when I got into the car they bowed low over their hands and in unison said "Salaam Missahib." Dhil Mahommad turned away quickly. He wiped his eyes on his sleeve. I even saw the sweeper on his own peering round a tree. He too gave me a salaam which I made a point of acknowledging.

At the railway station Ethel became more and more agitated. She repeatedly gave me all sorts of unnecessary instructions. I gave her a big hug and moved away. I was too full up for words as I knew what my leaving meant to her. Clive stood quietly and impassively in the background. When I went to kiss him goodbye he gave me an envelope. "Goodbye, child," he said accepting my kiss. "You're a grand girl and I'm sure you'll make out." He turned and left the platform quickly. Ethel was alone, crying unashamedly as the train chuffed out of the station taking me to a far off place and, she thought, probably out of her life. I was alone in the two berth carriage and as the train chugged through the green rice fields I sat on my bunk and opened the letter from Clive. There was a cheque for £200. I knew it was a lot of money, but I had no idea of its purchasing value and I silently thanked my quiet reserved father. The thought of Ethel bothered me. I felt bad at leaving her. Damn these awful decisions. Damn this bloody war making life so urgent and difficult. Then I thought of Peter and the telegram I sent him. I worried that I hadn't said enough and that he might not be 'there', wherever 'there' is, to meet me.

I looked out of the window. The water buffalos plodded slowly through the damp fields, a thin man with his dhoti hitched up steering the plough. A group of small children carried bundles on their heads or tied to the end of sticks and walked single file along the raised path. All of them moved with grace. Large heavy birds circled slowly. The tranquillity of the scene calmed me. How I love this wide, grubby, smelly, exciting country. I mustn't dwell on thoughts of Shillong but I must think of the future and who will be waiting for me at the end of the journey. I changed stations and crossed Calcutta under the guidance of Clive's friend. The seething traffic and myriads of people that I had seen on my first journey were now competing for road space with all the military vehicles, huge American ten-tonners and whizzing dispatch riders. I settled comfortably into the broad gauge carriage with two other people for the three night journey across the wide continent. They were sisters, both mousey and self-effacing. They had little luggage and seemed happy to sit on a lower bunk and talk in whispers to each other. They spoke to me only when I addressed them. It was all very different from the bewilderment I suffered on the outward journey. I didn't feel embarrassed eating meals in the station restaurants while the Indian people sat and waited. I looked at crippled children and it didn't upset me. I realised I had become hard and uncaring like the rest of the Europeans resident permanently in India. Perhaps we all grew a veneer so as not to take the suffering to heart. I couldn't call England 'home' like most people out here do. Perhaps it would seem like home when we settled somewhere, just me and Peter. I wished I could shut my eyes and simply arrive and be married. The train rumbled on and on. Each time it stopped for the first class passengers to have their dinner, I posted a letter to Shillong. They would probably take ten days to arrive. I hoped they would help Ethel to cheer up. The transfer from train to ship went smoothly in Bombay. The S.S. Oriental was much bigger than the S.S. Terne. It was a passenger liner converted to a troop carrier. The soldiers had already embarked: thousands of them passing the time away on the lower decks. I was led down several stairways to my cabin. What a disappointment! It wasn't cabin at all, just a converted corridor without a porthole so there was no clean air. The bunks were in tiers of four on either side. There was not enough space to sit up. Although I knew I was to travel second class I hadn't expected these conditions. We each had a small locker with a padlock and key and one coat hook for coats. All our other luggage had to be put in a store room. I settled for a top bunk and made myself as organised as possible in preparation for the three week voyage. The blackout regulations were still very strict. I found my way to the Purser's office to ask for the whereabouts of my future employers, Brigadier and Mrs Henderson. "They've just boarded, Miss," a large bellied man informed me. "In Stateroom three. Top Deck. First right up the gangway." I marvelled at their accommodation, real beds, space, cupboards and two windows, real windows, not portholes. The Hendersons greeted me perfunctorily. The Brigadier was short and stuffy. My first instincts were of distaste for he looked like a cold, old codfish. Mrs Henderson peered round behind him, flustered and anxious and pregnant. "Here are the children," she said. "Jane, Jack, and Annabel, seven, five and three. And there's Jasper, he's just one. He's the one I want you to look after."

"He looks a dear little boy," I said politely. Inwardly I recognised a child who had been spoilt and pampered by the Indian ayah. He rushed round the cabin on all fours, knocking aside what got in his way.

"When do you want me to start?" I asked.

Mrs Henderson prattled on, "As I'm pregnant again I can't do as much as usual and the heat bothers me. Now, this is what I want you to do. Go with the children to their meal sittings. The older ones shouldn't be any bother. And of course, keep an eye on Jasper when he's awake."

"I'll try," I said, "but you'll have to show me how to put on a nappy."

"Gracious me, girl. Fancy you not knowing how to do that." Mrs Henderson snorted, which irritated me. "And we want you to do all the washing. You can do that while Jasper has his sleep and the others are in the day nursery. Then..."

"When shall I start?" I interrupted, anxious to get on deck and find my way around.

Mrs Henderson took no notice. "We shall pay you a pound a week pocket money," she continued. She paused, waiting for my reactions. I was so bewildered that I gave her none. "I gather you're getting a free passage," she said in a withering tone. "Now, please take Jasper on deck while I sort myself out and have a rest."

The next half hour was a nightmare. Jasper crawled here and there, yelled when I tried to pick him up and wiggled in my arms. I felt like smacking his bottom and wondered how I'd be feeling at the end of the voyage. He tried to climb the furniture and stairs and I was glad the ship was stationary. That night, slightly daunted at the prospect of the three weeks ahead, I lay trying to sleep and heard the rhythm of the engines. I crawled down from my top bunk, trying to be quiet and put on what day clothes I could find. Then I went on deck and breathed cool air. It was dawn as the ship pulled away from the quay and made a sedate journey through the tiny boats whose owners were waiting hopefully to sell last-minute purchases to the passengers. Only a few soldiers were up so trade was slow. I watched the land that I had grown to love gradually fade away and felt a twinge of sadness. The small lights flickered and then disappeared as the dawn became daylight. Bicycles and riders appeared from all corners of the narrow streets and wobbled their journey through the crowds. I saw cattle moving slowly and children on the way to school before the heat became too great. I saw women with baskets on their heads all getting smaller, smaller, further and further away as the ship sailed steadily out to sea. Then there was a blur of the coastline, then just a horizon. I looked at my watch. It was nearly 7 o'clock. Telling myself to pull myself together and not get depressed I rushed to my bunk space and tried to sort out some clothes. Most of the others were sleeping. I went up to the top deck and knocked at the Henderson's door. Jasper was dressed and ready for breakfast. He was cross and murmured baby language. In the adjacent cabin I heard the other children struggling into their clothes. We were the first down to breakfast. The stewards were only just ready. The stale smell in the dining saloon was horrid. Nannies and children were seated at a long table, highly polished but with no table cloth. The other tables all had clean white cloths and their own salt, peppers and sugars. Jasper sat in a high chair, waving his spoon and shouting. I tried to shovel cereal into his mouth but most of it went down his bib. I drunk orange juice and ate some toast. After breakfast I watched Jasper till 10.30 when he went to sleep in his cot, his nappy all sixes and sevens. While he slept I made my first attempt at washing. The horror of the facilities soon dawned on me. We were only allocated one basin of fresh water to each family, and in that I had to wash all the clothes for seven. Everything, even the nappies, had to be rinsed out in hot salt water. Apart from the horrible smell, the soap never came out properly. Soon the clothes themselves began to smell and Mrs Henderson complained. "Your washing's not much good, Emma. The dhobi could do better with his cold water and stone."

I bit my tongue and moved Jasper to the other hip. "I'm having to use salt water for rinsing. And the communal drying room is smelly too," I countered. She tut tutted and left the cabin. She had begun to annoy me with her superior airs. I beavered through the long days, thankful for the time when Jasper was in his cot tucked up for the night and the older children were looking at books on their bunks. Supper time was fun. The food was typical stodgy mass pro- duced stuff for people with large appetites. The non-commissioned officers and wives were lively companions and agreeable to talk with. As my evenings were free I went up to the top deck groping for the railings. I didn't want to make conversation in hot smokey rooms. There was not a glimmer of light from the ship, only the light of the moon and stars to steer by. I breathed in the sweet air of the tropical nights and dwelt in moments of nostalgia with Peter in Shillong. The swish of the bows through the water was soothing and rhythmic, the hordes of flying fish scuttering away dramatic. I felt I had a right to sit on the top deck as I spent most of my days there with the children. It was quieter than the lower decks and I enjoyed meeting the officers and their wives. I knew I looked hot and harassed during the day. Now it was so dark it didn't matter what I looked like. While sitting alone a certain Anthony made a point of talking to me. I enjoyed his company and his conversation. As we squeezed through the Suez Canal Anthony took the opportunity of squeezing my hand. The full moon made silver blue dancing beams in the water. Even in the day time everything that moved seemed to go at slow speed. The camels looked like fleas strolling on a hair. Patterns of the dunes were ever changing as the sun or moon ranged across the sky. Anthony made me feel womanly and happy, a contrast to the Henderson family, but I had to keep him at arm's length, tact- fully explaining my relationship with Peter. The Hendersons proved curt and arrogant. There was no rapport with the three older children and Jasper was a nightmare; so I moved through each day like an automaton. But once there was a difference. After the children's session for supper I laid the laundry into tidy piles on the bunks ready to put into drawers. Jasper played on the floor of the cabin, strewing his toys everywhere. When it was silent, I turned round to look for him; he wasn't there. In my panic I realised that the cabin door had opened, perhaps with the swell of the ship. I hunted all over, in the shower, in the airing room, in the washrooms. Up and down the passage, even poking my head in to some other cabins. But there was no sign of Jasper. I knew I couldn't possibly tell that damned woman that I'd lost her baby. For well over fifteen minutes I hunted high and low, sweating under the arm pits and cursing. I felt sure that he couldn't have reached the outside because of the high step and heavy door leading to the deck. But in desperation I went to have a look. I pushed the heavy outside door open, and climbed over the high step. I looked forward, nothing. Then I looked aft. "Jasper, Jasper," I called. "Come back, quick. Come back." I saw him with his head and shoulders underneath the bottom rung of the railings watching the waves. The only thing that was stopping him from sliding overboard with the roll of the ship was the badly tied and bulky nappy which I had put on. "You bad, bad, boy," I scolded. Jasper laughed. "But thank God, you're safe."

Anthony laughed long and loud when I told him the story in the evening, but I never told the Hendersons that I'd nearly lost their hateful baby. The three-week voyage went quickly. No U-boat attacks, no air attacks and a calm Bay of Biscay made the journey uneventful. It was the stuffiness of the ghastly sleeping quarters and the horrid Henderson family that made it unpleasant. I sensed a heaviness in Anthony as we sailed north, the Irish coast on our port side. I knew I'd miss our long conversations and his manly company. As he kissed me gently on the lips he said, "Good-bye, my very special Emma. I shall remember this journey for a long time. Thank you for just being yourself." Then he turned and walked away and I didn't see him again. I felt saddened but knew that I would soon be seeing Peter and all would be well. The ship slowly steamed into Liverpool Harbour. I felt strangely elated yet nervous. The shape and colour of the buildings looked unfamiliar. Many ships were in harbour and all of them needed a good coat of paint. The air was heavy and wet, and it smelt of fish and salt. The noise was subdued, just a few hoots from the small busy boats plying the wide strip of harbour water. Night fell as we anchored and darkness surrounded us. I had a sense of foreboding. Early the next morning I held Jasper in my arms and watched the few people on the quayside. I looked for Peter, but was not anxious that there was yet no sign of him. With so many troops on board I wondered why there were not more families waiting, excited and happy to greet the returning service men. "Not many people are there?" I asked at random to a fellow passenger who was standing alongside. "How could anyone know where and when to expect the boat when there's so much security around? My family don't know if I'm arriving at Southampton, Glasgow, London or here. They just about know I'll be turning up at the end of the month."

"My fiance seemed to think he'd be able to meet the boat. In fact he promised me." Panic waves started. I turned to look at my fellow passenger but he'd walked away. Disembarkation started quickly. The Hendersons were given priority and were met by a staff car and a three-ton lorry for their luggage. I looked after Jasper till they were ready to leave, then carried him down the gangway. I handed the baby to Mrs Henderson as they were about to climb into the car. They drove away with the minimum of thanks. Inwardly I fumed. What terrible people, I thought. Never even asked me if I was alright. Never offered help or advice. Hope I never get like that. I climbed slowly back up the gangway scanning the small crowd for Peter's blond head. I went to my bunk to make sure everything was ready and carried my possessions up on deck. Passengers and soldiers were streaming down the gangway. They were swallowed up in a huge shed and lost to my view. The ship was getting emptier and quieter. Why don't you come for me, Peter? What shall I do, where shall I go? It was five o'clock and I was still at the railings looking, waiting, when the Purser approached me.

Part 3

"It's time to go, Miss. It's time to go." The purser kept repeating himself. He was an elderly man with a paunch but he seemed to understand. "It ain't no good waiting. It isn't anyone's fault. Everythin's all kept secret. I'll get customs to clear your luggage and phone for a taxi. You're last on board so there won't be no delay."

"I was expecting my fiance." I felt I had to tell everyone. "I'm not really sure what to do or where to go but thank you all the same."

I went through customs without any delay. Chalk marks had been put on my luggage. The taxi driver was waiting. He was a friend of the purser and he had told him of my plight.

"I suggest you make straight for London," he said, "most of them do."

We scanned the timetable that was displayed alongside the taxi rank. There were no more trains that night.

"Seems you're in a bit of a muddle, Miss. What about leaving your luggage in the left luggage and finding a room for the night? Things'll look better in the morning. My daughter goes to the hostel for the night when she's stuck. She's in the Wrens. I'll take you to the hostel. You won't get rooked there."

"Thank you so much," was all I could think of to say. I felt lost and so alone.

The taxi drew up outside a large red brick building. The windows were protected by railings and steps led up to a heavy wooden door. A formidable desk stood at the end of a long tiled corridor.

"How much do I pay you?" I asked the taxi driver. I was beginning to panic. Everything was so different to India. Should I tip him and, if so, how much? Would a brown note be enough?

"Never mind about a tip, Miss, the brown note will be fine." I could have hugged him for making things so easy for me. I turned my back on him and made my way to the desk. A stout man in a tight uniform glared at me. "What d'you want?"

"Have you a bed for the night?"

He handed me a red ticket. "Bed 14," he said, "first ward on left. Cocoa at ten. Lights out 10.30. Breakfast 7.30. Pay first. Two bob."

I handed him a pound note. He looked disgruntled as he rummaged round for change.. I walked along to the ward and started to search for bed 14. It was at the end of a long room which had fifteen beds on each side. There was very little space between them. I hadn't expected my arrival to be like this. I was too tired and unhappy to think of cocoa or supper. I pulled the grubby blanket over my legs and fell asleep almost immediately. I woke at midnight with a blinding headache. It was migraine. I knew I had to reach a bathroom quickly. I felt sick. I reached the lavatories just in time and I threw up. I ended in a sweat with my head throbbing. I spent the rest of the night sitting on my bed with my head in my hands or making emergency dashes for the lavatory. I longed for a hot water bottle and for Peter to be there to help me.. I felt too ill to even think about getting to London.

The morning arrived at last. I sipped strong tea and felt a little better. I walked slowly to the station.. It took an hour but I enjoyed the fresh air. My headache went as quickly as it had come. I decided to take the ten o'clock train to Kings Cross and make up my mind what to do when I got there. If only I could phone Peter but I didn't know where he was. The train was filling up, mainly with men and women in uniform. I managed to find a corner seat and settled down for the journey. I didn't have anything to read or eat on the journey and didn't know how to go about getting anything. There were no boys with trays on their heads selling anything and everything like there were in India.

Away from the town, the grass looked emerald green and primroses were scattered along the banks. Tiny lambs skipped in the meadows and the cattle looked sleek and shiny, so different to the cows in Calcutta. The countryside presented such a different picture to the sun scorched plains of India. I sat through that journey trying to press away the despair that knocked at my heart. I didn't know what I was going to do. The train moved slowly into Kings Cross and I saw the bomb damage, the roofless houses and shattered buildings, flat spaces where wild flowers had taken root and softened the broken outlines.

There was a general rush when the train stopped. People shoved and pushed in their haste to leave the carriage. I was the last to leave. I walked slowly to the goods van. My baggage was in a pile and I looked at it hesitatingly. The platform was empty except for one elderly, upright lady walking towards me. She held a photograph in her gloved hand. "Are you Emma?" she asked.

"Yes, I am but how did you know?"

"I'm Peter's mother. He sent us this photo of you some time ago."

I looked at it and saw that it was the one I had given him soon after we had met.

"But how did you know I'd be on this train?"

"My dear, it was the strangest thing. Peter is sick with worry. He's still up in the north of Scotland and can't get away but Sir Aubrey has ways of finding things out and he learned that your ship was due in soon and then I had this dream last night that told me to come and meet the ten o'clock train from Liverpool and here I am and I've found you."

I stared at her.

"Come along," she said, "Peter says you're to stay with us in Westminster until he phones. Is that alright dear?"

"Yes, of course." I was ashamed that my feelings were so apparent. Lady White dealt with the luggage. A taxi appeared. She managed everything so effortlessly. Peter had been right in his description of her. Her black fur coat and cheeky hat were faultless, her gloves, silk stockings and handbag looked new. I worried that this immaculate person who dreamed dreams and acted on them was going to be my mother-in-law. I felt a wreck beside her. I had no thin stockings and my shoes felt like mountain boots. My coat was the one I had worn at school and so were most of the other clothes in my luggage. I began to wish I could hide.

The Whites had a suite of rooms in The Hermis Hotel in Westminster. Lady Olivia lead the way to the sitting room, graciously thanking the lift attendant. The room was large and bright. There were two large upholstered chairs with several small tables, a cupboard with glasses and a few bottles and a wireless. I looked at my future father-in-law. I had never seen a man like Sir Aubrey. He was huge. A great head with tender eyes bent towards me. He wore a tweed suit with a matching waistcoat, a gold chain dangling from an inner pocket.

"Well, so this is Emma. I'm really proud to meet you, coming all this way for my son. Well done, well done. Old Peter seems to have chosen a smasher. What do you say, Olly?"

Lady Olivia turned her head to one side and smiled. Sir Aubrey took my hand and led me across to the gas fire and showed me where to sit, then he sat down beside me. "And that son of mine couldn't get down to meet you, too bad, too bad. The old folks will have to make it up to you. We'll look after you and arrange everything. Peter's up north and it's difficult to contact him. I'll pull what strings I can and see that he phones you as soon as possible."

I felt the love, kindness and authority of the man sweep over me.

"It's very kind of you both," I stammered. "I'd be lost without your advice," and then suddenly, responding to a spontaneous impulse, I whispered into Sir Aubrey's ear, "and I hope Peter grows into someone like you."

He replied with a wink while Lady Olivia looked at her watch.

"Emma dear," she said, "it's unfortunate but we've a business dinner at The Dorchester tonight. It's to do with Sir Aubrey's project in Egypt. We think it would be best if you came along with us. Now dear, go and have a bath and a rest and be ready for dinner at seven. I'll ring up to you when we're ready to go."

I wondered what 'be ready' meant. I only had my Indian cotton dresses with me and they wouldn't be warm enough. The only alternative was my old school dress and that was tight across the bust.

I was shown a small room at the top of the hotel. It was clean and warm and had a telephone beside the bed. I sat on the bed and tried to collect my thoughts. There was a knock on the door and I called, "Come in."

A dark suited man stood in the doorway. I recoiled from him. "Go away," I shouted. "I'm not that sort of girl."

"But I'm only the valet, miss. I've come to see if there's anything you need ironing." He closed the door with a sniff of disdain.

I took a long, hot bath and marvelled at the unlimited hot water and warm fluffy towels. It was so different to the tin tubs and buckets of water from the Pine Lodge days. I squeezed into my high necked school dress and put on the only pair of lisle stockings I possessed but they felt thick and ugly. Even my shoes could have been worn to climb Everest. I brushed my hair until it shone and dusted powder on my nose. I hoped the Whites would not be too ashamed of me. I longed for Peter. If it hadn't been for him, I would have run a mile.

Lady Olivia appeared dressed in a short black velvet dress with a double string of pearls sitting in the boat shaped neck. She had a small cape of curly black fur slung over one shoulder. She looked at me and commented, "We'll have to take you shopping tomorrow, must have you looking nice for the wedding. But my de....ar (she managed to prolong the vowel) haven't you any other footwear?"

"No, Lady Olivia," I stuttered, "and I'm very short of winter clothes."

Sir Aubrey ushered us out to the taxi. The short drive to The Dorchester should have been a delight but I was too nervous to appreciate the new surroundings. We swept up the circular entrance to the hotel where a red coated man took Lady Olivia's arm and lead her to the revolving doors. He had rows of medals on his chest. Sir Aubrey paid the taxi and then he guided me. It was all splendour inside the revolving doors. The men wore dinner jackets. Most of the ladies had small fur jack-

Sir Aubrey

ets or capes. Diamonds sparkled. A few tiaras gleamed. Brittle laughter filled the air. Sir Aubrey found the corner where his friends were collecting and drinks were passed round. When they were all assembled, Lady Olivia made an an-

47

nouncement.

"Ladies and Gentlemen," she said, "before we go into dinner, I would like to introduce you to Emma. She is my daughter-in-law to be and has just arrived from India this morning. She is going to marry my younger son, Peter."

I felt so embarrassed but Sir Aubrey came to my rescue. He put his arm round my shoulder and said, "I think she is the most beautiful girl in the world. Just look at her eyes. It's no wonder Peter couldn't live without her. She's been very brave travelling across the seas in these conditions."

We were ushered into the dining room and the meal continued without disaster but there was so much pretension and ceremony that it seemed to go on for ever. A three piece band played at end of the hall . Lights blazed behind the velvet curtains. The war seemed a long way away.

"Well done de...ar, you did very well," Lady Olivia said as we waited in the spacious hall for the doorman to call a taxi.

"You didn't expect her to eat off her knife, did you?" Sir Aubrey teased.

"At least you're not coffee coloured," Lady Olivia continued. "We weren't sure from the photo whether your eyes were brown or blue. We'll have breakfast at nine o'clock tomorrow, then we'll do some shopping."

I went straight up to my room as soon as I got back and cuddled down in my comfortable bed. I was just dozing off when the telephone rang.

"Hello, hello, hello. Is that Emma?" The voice crackled and sounded far away. "Emma, can you hear me?"

"Peter, it's you. Yes, I can hear you but you're crackly. I'm alright, yes, really."

"Emma darling, I don't know what to say. It's been so long. How did you manage to disembark? I've been so *worried*. Look, I'm getting a week's leave in a fortnight's time Think we can get married then, up here in Scotland. What's that. Damn this line."

"Yes, Peter, yes to everything. Write to me darling. It's better than this. I'll plan for two weeks. Let me know where. Oh damn those pips. Phone me tomorrow Peter."

"O.K. same time..." The line went dead.

Hearing Peter's voice like that put the events of the last few days into perspective. I hugged myself as I recalled over and over again every word that he had said until I fell asleep.

When coffee had been poured at breakfast the next morning and we were all settled, I said, "Peter phoned last night. It was very crackly so we couldn't say much. He's been given leave in a fortnight's time and wants us to get married then somewhere in Scotland. He's going to write it all down and phone again tonight. Will that be alright? It will be alright won't it, Sir Aubrey?" I had turned towards him because I thought he was my ally.

"Can't have you calling me Sir Aubrey. We'll settle for Father and Mother shall we? Yes, my dear, you just fix what you can with Peter. We'll come along to the wedding, that's if you ask us." Flushed with excitement, Sir Aubrey put an extra large dollop of marmalade on his toast.

"Steady with the marmalade, Aubrey. I told you last week that this pot had to last us for a month." Lady Olivia had to have the last word. "Well Emma, if Peter wants to marry you quickly, we must do our bit this end so we'll start shopping straight away. Funny sort of wedding this is going to be with no guest list and no presents and no bridesmaids. Who will want to travel all the way to Scotland for a wedding?"

"It's getting them together that counts," Sir Aubrey said calmly.

"That's how I feel, "I said in a quiet voice but Lady Olivia didn't seem to hear.

So the round of shopping began. Lady Olivia only used the well known stores and she herself seemed well known to the staff. She settled herself in at Debenhams. The assistants, the buyers, the floor manager, all of them fluttered around us. I felt helpless and lost amongst so much advice.

"You're rather large for most of the clothes," Lady Olivia pointed out tact-lessly. "My daughter, Vivienne, is about your size and she manages to look smart. Try this one on."

I slipped on one dress after another, never once looking at the price. They were all too short in length, too short waisted or just tight. I began to despair. Then I saw a pale green, long sleeved dress at the back of the rail.

"I'd like to try this one, "I said.

It fitted beautifully. A small drape across the midriff hid my hips and clever darting under my bosom gave me a sexy look. "I'd like this one, " I said. "I'd like to get married in it. I've got some gold shoes and brooch but what about a hat?"

"I don't know what would suit you with your short hair." Lady Olivia turned to the buyer. "Have you some material of this dress? If you have I'll make a hat. Don't worry, Emma. I'll make a hat that will make Peter proud of you."

The morning ended up with a dress at £15, a warm blue draped dress at £20 and a tailored suit for £25. It seemed an awful lot of money. On the way to Debenhams I'd seen clothes at half that price. I still had outdoor clothes and underclothes to buy out of the £200 as well as a present for Peter. Lady Olivia never asked about the price. If she wanted anything she bought it. I had a little money I had saved as well as the £200 but I wanted to keep that for emergen-cies. I was lucky in that I had received the tropical allowance of clothing cou-pons when I had returned to the U.K. so that wasn't a problem.

"We've done well for the first day, de....ar," Lady Olivia said. "I'm going to rest this afternoon. Do you think you could manage to get yourself some stock-ings and get yourself a haircut too. It's a bit shaggy even though it's short." I wondered if she realised how inferior she made me feel.

49

I walked across St. James Park and up Regents Street to Debenhams I found the hosiery department and asked the elderly assistant to show me what was available. She showed me some stockings at half a crown a pair.

"They look fine to me," I said relieved that it was so easy. Then I offered to buy them in the same way that I would have done in Shillong market. "I'll give you six shillings for three pairs. That's fair isn't it?"

The assistant pulled herself to her full height and managed to look down her nose at me. "We don't do that kind of thing here," she said and she turned and walked away.

I retreated to a small coffee shop in a back street. A tired old waitress took my order. I was puzzled that an old lady was waiting on me. In India all the servants were men except for the ayahs who looked after the babies. She returned in a few minutes carrying a really heavy tray. I was on my feet straight away. "Let me help you," I said. "It's far too heavy for you."

"Don't you dare touch it," she shouted. "Trying to get my job are you? You go and sit down and mind your own business."

I was overwhelmed with embarrassment. I drank my tea quickly and then made another attempt to buy the necessary stockings. I didn't dare face Lady Olivia with empty hands.

That night, Peter phoned again. The line was clearer and I started to pour out my troubles.

"Emmy love, listen to me first. I've got so many plans. Can you come up to Comrie in Perthshire on Friday? That's just five days away and can you arrange to marry me on the following Saturday week? That's Saturday, 28th of April. Ask the old folks will you? We'll have the whole weekend together so we can talk. Are you there love?"

"Yes, I'm here darling. It's all coming so suddenly I can hardly take it all in."

"We can change it if you want to."

"Me? Want to change my wedding after waiting all this time, never."

"I want you to have a good hard look at me darling. You may find I've changed and I'm not the man you want to marry. I want you to be honest with me."

"How can you say such a thing?" I was distraught and felt my world crumbling. "Peter, don't do this to me."

"I know it sounds strange love, but you were the one that had the doubts. I knew from the first minute I saw you that I wanted you for my wife. Explain everything to Mum and Dad. Try and get your Aunt Mathilda to come and what about Di?"

The pips went. "I'll phone again tomorrow" silence. The line had gone dead.

I went downstairs and knocked on the White's door.

"Can I come in for a minute?" I asked. "Peter's just phoned again."

They were both in their dressing gowns.

"Peter wants me to travel up to Comrie on Friday and he's planning to fix the wedding for the 28th. He told me to ask you both specially to come but he wants me to have a look at him before I commit myself. Can you imagine it? Me. changing my mind after all this time?"

Sir Aubrey took charge of the situation straight away.

"We'll phone the station first thing in the morning and get your ticket booked. Then you can tell Peter what time you'll be arriving when he phones. Next time he phones, ask him where you're going to stay, can't have you arriving with nowhere to go."

I felt relief surging through my body. It was all going to be alright.

"Go to bed now. You've had a long day." Lady Olivia was dismissive as she plumped up the pillows and, sitting on the edge of the bed, let her fluffy slippers fall on to the floor.

"I'd like to visit an old school friend," I began.

"We'll see to it in the morning. Good night Emma, good night," and she pulled back the sheets.

"Good night, child," Sir Aubrey said and he blew me a kiss.

I climbed the stairs feeling bemused with the sudden turn of events. There was always tomorrow.

"I really must see Aunt Mathilda and Di," I said at breakfast the next morning. "They are two very special people that I loved when I was growing up. Perhaps I could persuade them to come to the wedding." I noticed Lady Olivia starting her heavy breathing.

"You go when you like, my dear," Sir Aubrey chipped in. "I'll explain the underground to you. And Emma, find time to write to your parents. They'll be so sad to miss your big day. I'm going to write to tell them how glad we are and that you're already one of the family. I'll send a telegram when we're sure of the dates."

"You've still got some things to do, you know. Getting married just doesn't happen," Lady Olivia was determined to get her oar in.

"I'd like to see Di this afternoon when she finishes work and go and see Aunt Mathilda tomorrow. Is it alright if I fix that with them?" I felt strong enough to argue the point with Lady Olivia if it proved necessary.

We shopped that morning and I was relieved when Lady Olivia said that she felt tired. I excused myself from lunch saying that I would like some fresh air. As I walked along the tow path from the tube station to the large block of flats at Hurlingham, I wondered if Di had changed from the frail little schoolgirl who loved to play the piano. I climbed the stairs to the fourth floor. I didn't dare trust myself to the lift and all the complicated buttons that had to be pressed. Mrs Turnball opened the door and immediately all the old memories came flooding back and my eyes began to smart.

"Emma, Emma," she exclaimed, "you haven't changed a bit," and she hugged me.

"Hi there, Emmy," and there was Di, immaculate, petite and full of bounce and energy, so different to the quiet little schoolgirl.

She came and stood beside me looking out of the window. I saw the chimneys of the power station and the battered houses across the river. It was low tide and the view was sad and a little grubby.

"Married in two weeks, Emmy, and you're still a baby. You're younger than me and I haven't got a permanent boyfriend."

Mrs Turnball came in carrying a tray with tea and biscuits."

"Any news from Italy yet?" I asked.

There was a slight pause, a slight tension.

"Yes," Di said. "We've heard from the Red Cross. A party of them escaped to Switzerland by walking over the Alps. Dad was older than the others and he's suffered most but they're safe and they're alive and that's the most important thing but it's hard on Mum, believe you me. It's the not knowing that tells on you. We didn't know if he was alive or dead for ages."

Mrs Turnball came in and poured the tea. I could see the tension in her face whenever we mentioned the war. After a while she pleaded that she had to do the ironing and left the two of us together.

"You must come to the wedding, Di. You'll be my only guest. Promise me you'll come. I'm getting all jittery and mother-in-law makes me worse. She makes such a fuss about everything."

"Of course I'm coming, Em. I must have a look at Peter and see if I approve of him. Wish I had someone to look after me."

I spent the next afternoon with Aunt Mathilda. We hugged long and hard and the gesture was meaningful. The house where I had lived on my holidays from school seemed so tiny. The garden where I had played was minuscule. Even Aunt Mathilda seemed smaller, but the smell of lavender was just the same. I asked her what had happened to Gertrude the maid and why was the grass in the orchard so long .

I drank tea out of the same dainty china cups and sat on the same mauve cushion and looked at the same portrait of the old man with a beard.

"It is good to see you, Aunt Mathilda. Are you well?"

I had noticed the fatigue lines on her face and the dark shadows beneath her eyes.

"Yes dear, I'm alright. Gertrude joined up you know. I do miss her being here when I get home. I'm working three days a week. The college don't seem to want me to give up. But let's talk about you? Married in Scotland in two weeks time? Have you a photo of Peter? I'm sorry Emma. It's too far away for me to come. I would have loved to be there but... Tell me about Pine Lodge. How are Clive and Ethel? Are they alright, really alright?"

I spent a long time telling her about life in Shillong. Then Aunt Mathilda went to a cupboard and fetched a brooch.

"This is for you dear from all my heart. May you have all the happiness you deserve. God bless you and your new man." We walked together to the station. We didn't need to talk. The rapport between us was mutual despite the difference in our ages. When we reached the station, Aunt Mathilda said, "Don't say anything more dear. The train won't be long. I'll leave you at the entrance." She turned away and walked slowly back the way we had come. She looked so lonely and forlorn. I determined that I would take Peter to see her.

The rest of the week was spent in a whirlwind of shopping. Lady Olivia tried to organise every minute of my day but I managed to slip away by myself to buy Peter a present, a pair of ivory backed hair brushes engraved with the regimental crest in black.

I was packed and ready long before I was due to leave for the train on Friday. As it didn't leave until 10pm I paced the floor and worried. I wondered if I was still good enough for him or if he had found somebody else. I worried about where we would live after we were married. I worried about our first night as man and wife for I knew nothing whatsoever about sex. I was getting into a real frenzy when Sir Aubrey phoned up to say that the taxi was waiting..

The Whites took me to the station and found the first class berth that had been reserved for me. Sir Aubrey tipped the attendant and I was surprised at the amount of the tip. The train door slammed and I peered through the window.

"I'll see you next Friday. You'll be sure to have the hat won't you mother? Thank you for all you've done. I'll miss you both. Goodbye and thank you." Sir Aubrey stayed waving his large handkerchief until I was out of sight.

When the train arrived at Edinburgh, a porter knocked on my door and said that he had been told to look after me. I told him I had to get a train to Crieff and phone to say what time it would arrive.

"You'd best go and get some breakfast at the hotel then, Miss," he said. "The train leaves for Crieff at 10.30 and arrives at 12.30. I'll look after your luggage. Be back here at ten and don't be late."

"That won't be likely," I said with a laugh.

Peter was out when I phoned but I left a message. Then I had my first Scottish meal, a bowl of porridge with added salt and new baps, hot coffee with saccharin and plenty of milk to follow.

I felt good in my new suit. I knew I would treasure these moments of anticipation for the rest of my life. The porter told me the luggage was already in the guard's van and that was it. I was on the last leg of my journey. I looked out of the window and felt my eyes shining and my lips quivering with excitement. An old lady dressed in black was sitting opposite me. "Excuse me, dearie," she interrupted my thoughts, "do you mind me commenting on your appearance. You've got such a light in your eyes."

"I'm just so happy," I told her. "I'm going to meet the man I'm going to marry and I haven't seen him for ages."

"What a lovely story. You make the most of every good minute while you have them. Sometimes they don't last that long."

I realised then that she was in black.

"Yes, my dear. I'm wearing black in honour of my three boys. I lost them all within a year but seeing you looking so happy has made me realise that there is a glimpse of hope in the world. You have all my best wishes and my prayers."

"Thank you," I said , "and I'm so sorry." I wished that my precious moments hadn't been shattered by the sadness of this elderly lady. Did happiness always run in tandem with sadness?

The train drew slowly into Crieff station and there was Peter, his blonde hair half hidden by his glengarry, tapping his knee with his cane and looking anxiously up and down.

"I'm here, Peter," I called out.

"Go now and God be with you," the old lady said as I jumped on to the platform. I stood there shivering. I couldn't move.

"Hey darling, what's up? You're shaking."

"Oh Peter, at last."

He gave me a quick kiss and a cuddle and in a low voice he added, "I don't like kissing in uniform but I'll make it up to you later. Come on, I've been allocated a jeep so show me where your luggage is."

We sat, fingers entwined as we were driven through the town.

"Emma, this is my right hand man, Melville, my batman," Peter said, pointing towards the driver. I sensed that the officer and batman had a wonderful rapport.

"I met you once in Shillong," I said, "but I don't expect you remember. I've only had good reports about you and I'm very pleased to know that you're looking after this man."

"Thank you, ma'am. The major's been in a right state these last few weeks about your return. Glad you made it ma'am. We'll look after you." He continued driving looking straight ahead all the time.

He turned into a carpark beside a small, grey stone hotel. All the houses in the road were built of the same grey stone.

"I've booked you in here, Em and reserved a double for Mum and Dad next weekend. I've got to live in the Mess. Melville, take the heavy luggage back to the lines. I'll be walking back, so I won't need you again this evening "

Melville saluted and drove off.

Two little elderly sisters fussed around us, making me sign the visitors' book in a room that was only big enough for a desk and two chairs. They both wore grey skirts and grey cardigans. The taller sister wore a pink jumper while the other wore a blue one. We passed stuffed animal heads as we climbed the stairs and a fish tank with immobile fish hung among false ferns. I could feel Peter grinning as he followed the three of us upstairs.

"Dinner is at seven," the taller sister said.

"And water comes hot about six."

"Cups of tea at four o'clock."

"It's so nice to have you with us."

"Everything's fine. Thank you so much." I wished that they would go.

"We'll see you at seven then." The door shut with a click and suddenly we were alone together and in those few seconds all those wasted moments were pushed aside.

"Emma, Emma," Peter said softly, "Your eyes, your beautiful eyes," and he kissed them gently. I had no words. We sat there holding hands and, suddenly, the flood gates opened and the words poured out in torrents. Words of hope, of plans, of love. Words of commitment, words of advice. Then long, gentle, loving embraces but there was none of the fiery passion that we had felt in Shillong. We had the future before us and the urgency had disappeared, instead there was a deepness, a tenderness, a oneness........

We missed afternoon tea but went in together for dinner. We sat at a table in the corner but all eyes turned to look at us. After the meal we went out to the hills at the back of the village. The evening stayed light and it was deliciously cool. We walked along a lane scattered with pink and white flowers and primroses, masses of primroses.

"Emmy darling. I'm going to ask you again. Just because you've come all this way, it doesn't mean you can't say no. Are you sure that you haven't changed your mind. Am I still the person you fell in love with? Do you think you can manage with me for ever?" He took my hand and put it to his lips.

"How can you ask such a thing? I've never had any doubts. Is this your way of saying you don't want to marry me?"

"Oh gracious! If only you knew what I've been through wanting you, waiting..." He took me in his arms and pressed his lips hard over mine. We kissed long and tenderly, touching all the way down. I felt Peter harden and he knew that I had felt him.

"And now," he said, "I'm going to take you back to the hotel," and when I started to protest, he added, "and you know very well why."

"We dawdled down the hill and Peter paused again. "Em, there's one thing we haven't discussed and it's a big subject and a difficult one. It's about a family. Have you thought about having a baby? There's nothing more in this world I would love after you than to have a son."

The directness of his question knocked me sideways. "I don't know Peter, I just don't know. I'm so ignorant on that side of things. You'll have to help me but, Peter, I would like to feel a bit more settled. Everything's happening so fast. We've no home and..."

"O.K. precious, enough said. I can see you're apprehensive. On the contraceptive side, I took the bull by the horns and wrote off to a firm which supplies the necessary equipment for women. It should come next week."

The week went by too quickly. There was so much to do. Peter worked all day and I felt a little lost in the daytime. Some of the other officers' wives popped in for a chat but most of them had children and couldn't stay long. We drank tea with the priest who was going to marry us. He seemed a little bewildered and rather vague. " I hope he'll remember the service," I said to Peter.

"He'll know it backwards," Peter laughed. "Now what about the flowers Em? Have you managed to arrange anything?"

"Di and I will do those on Friday. They're all ordered."

"The Mess sergeant is seeing to the reception. There'll be about sixty of us."

"Sixty," I stopped in my tracks and stared at him. "That many? I thought we were going to have a small wedding. I won't know anyone."

Peter in training

"Don't worry love. It's going to be a happy day. We'll all be there to support you."

We walked back to the hotel and found the post had arrived and there was a small parcel for me. The contraceptives had turned up. I decided to open them on my own .I put them on one side and waited until Peter had left. There were only instructions for the woman in the packet. I presumed Peter would have his own. The instructions said the white tablets that were included should be inserted before intercourse. I wondered where I should insert them. Then I found a rubber balloon with a nozzle and yards of tubing. I was to insert the nozzle up my vagina, attach the tube to a tap and rinse gently. I found it more and more puzzling. I shoved it all back in the box and decided to wait until Di arrived. She might understand it better than me.

Friday arrived and I went in the jeep with Melville to meet Di. It was lovely to see her again. We giggled over lunch and while we were arranging the flowers in the church. The Whites arrived before dinner and I introduced Di. Dinner went smoothly and to mark the special occasion, we had candles on the table. The ceremony of trying on the hat took place after dinner while Di and I were on our own when we were supposed to be powdering our noses.

"You've picked a winner," Di said as we went upstairs. "Peter's just like his Dad."

I brought out the hat.

"Oh," said Di." I can't call that a winner. Look at the stuffed birds. Oh Em!" It wouldn't stay on my head. "It'll be alright tomorrow, " Di said, "we'll hold it in place with grips."

"Is it alright?" Lady Olivia asked when we went back downstairs. "Why didn't you wear it for us to see?"

"I didn't want Peter to see it," I lied.

"We'll all see it tomorrow," Sir Aubrey soothed. "Now I think an early night for us all. It will be a long day tomorrow. Peter, my boy, we'll see you in the Church and I'll be the proudest man there walking up the aisle to give this lovely girl to you."

"Well said," Di said firmly.

Peter, Di and I talked into the early hours of the morning.

"I really must go. See you at Church tomorrow. My goodness it's tomorrow today."

"Lucky you," Di said sleepily.

"But Di, do look at this", and I took the package out from beneath my underclothes. What am I supposed to do with it?"

"I dunno," Di said grinning from ear to ear. "The only man I ever had put something on himself."

"Heigh ho," I said, "another problem to solve but Whoopee for this time tomorrow."

"Lucky blighter," Di said quietly.

The great day arrived and the morning went in a haze. We had a quick sandwich for lunch and I began to dress. I slipped the pale green frock over my head and it slithered down my body. It felt good but then there was the question of face, hair and hat.

"Di, whatever shall I do? Look at my hair. It's gone all frizzy and this stupid hat."

"Never mind," Di soothed me down. "It's not that bad. If you tuck that bit in there and fix it with a grip, there you are. That's better. Remember that it'll please the old lady."

"You are irreverent Di and I love you for it. I've got the jitters, that's what's the matter."

I bent down to try on my old gold dancing pumps.

"Em, those shoes! They don't suit the dress. Haven't you any others?"

"No I haven't," I snapped. "I spent my coupons on other things. Don't say they're awful or I'll be thinking of them all the time."

"No-one will notice," Di said. "I'll be right behind you. Remember this is your big day. Come on, let's go down."

I fiddled with Aunt Mathilda's brooch, pinning it on my left shoulder. It

Church in Comrie 1944

gave me a sense of continuity in a whirlwind day.

Lady Olivia was waiting resplendent in mauve silk with a diamond choker. She looked me up and down and I felt like a horse being vetted for sale. "It looked nicer in the shop," she muttered. Much to my surprise she kissed me on the cheek. It knocked my hat crooked again. Sir Aubrey was full of emotion. He could only stutter and stammer. We squeezed into the hired car and set off. The hotel staff stood on the steps and gave us a small cheer as we set off.

It was only minutes later that I found myself walking up the aisle on Sir Aubrey's arm. He squeezed my hand as much for his own assurance as mine. I could sense from his breathing that he was near to tears. One side of the church was full of uniformed men singing their heads off. Di was on the other side

waiting and then there was Peter looking so smart and startlingly handsome in his Mess kit. We stood side by side at the altar rail and I followed my part of the service as if I was in a dream. Di stepped forward and took my flowers. I knelt beside Peter and whispered my vows in a haze as if it was someone else talking and I wasn't there at all but Peter was there beside me, warm, real and smelling a little of hot cloth. He was reassuring and steadfast and that was all that mattered. The piper played as we left church. It sent shivers down my spine but, in spite of the shivers, I felt an enormous sense of pride.

We were alone in the staff car, the faithful Melville at the wheel.

"Emmy, you're mine, all mine. You look terrific. This is going to be the best part because now I can show you off. Just be your happy self, precious and everyone will love you."

The reception was in the garden of the big house that had been commandeered for the officers' Mess. The sun shone and the pipers played in the orchard, eerie, exciting sounds. There were so many new faces and new names to remember. Sir Aubrey and Lady Olivia held court. Food was abundant. Champagne was abundant and Di was won-

derful. Whenever I felt flustered, she was there to smooth the situation.

"Cross your fingers and wish me luck," Peter said. "I'm going to make a speech." It was the usual list of thankyous. After the toasts had been drunk, I sneaked off to find the Mess sergeant and thank him personally.

"Glad to do it, Ma'am. The pleasure's ours. It's an honour to serve the major." I didn't know what else to do so I shook his hand. The sergeant stood to attention. Then I hurried back to the reception. Di was looking for me and hurried me upstairs to change. While I was changing into my blue draped dress, Lady Olivia came into the room. I tried to thank her for all her help but she said, "Don't try to thank me, dear. I was glad to help especially with your own mother so far away. But, Emma, look after him. He's very pre-

cious to me." She took my hand in hers and patted it. Her lips trembled and she went out without another word.

"Can't say anything , Di," I said. "I might cry."

I met Peter in the hall. He had changed into mufti, a kilt, long socks and a green sweater. I had never seen him dressed like that. He had always

worn tropical clothing in India. We ran the gauntlet of the cheering men, ducking beneath an arch of swords. When we got to the car, I ran back to Sir Aubrey for a last word. I reached up to whisper in his ear, "Thank you, thank you. I think you know what I mean. I'll look after him. I promise you. I'll always do my best."

"Go on, child, hurry," He reached for his handkerchief and blew his nose. It was very red.

Melville drove us to a large hotel on Loch Tuan. He had been sworn to secrecy. Whenever I looked at him, he was smiling. The hotel was a sombre, grey stoned building on the edge of the loch. Wood fires burned in all the main rooms. We were shown into the main suite. Now we were on our own, really on our own.

"Used to come here as a child," Peter said as he lifted the cases on to the rack, "and they remembered me. Look Em, the daffodils have arrived. They're my mother's favourite flower."

"It's all perfect Peter." I suddenly felt very tired. I looked out of the window, at the grey water and the pine trees and the sky and I suddenly felt unutterably alone. Then Peter put his arms round me. "Let me love you Emmy now, this minute."

With gentle hands and gentle words, Peter lead me through the mysteries of my first sexual experience and it was wonderful. Even through the hurt, I felt safe.

"My love, my love," Peter murmured. "Are you alright? Did it hurt?"

I didn't know how to answer. It had hurt but I didn't want to hurt him. I answered with a kiss. I knew Peter would never cause me pain and making love did hurt, I worried about it and wondered if I should tell him of the pain but I would cuddle into his warm body and feel comforted. As time went on, the hurt went.

I was woken that first morning by Peter's kiss.

"Had a good sleep, love? Come on. We've got so much to do. We've got the whole day ahead of us and so many plans. Have a bath now and we'll go down for breakfast and decide what we're going to do."

I found myself covered with embarrassment at undressing in front of Peter. He noticed my shyness and pretended to turn to shave. I felt better once I was in the bath.

The hot water and the smell of the honey and almond soap and Peter's after shave gave me a feeling of grandeur. I could hear him chuckle and hum. Life seemed so right.

Peter's enthusiasm for everything infected me. We walked across hills. We fished in the loch. We looked for young grouse. Peter seemed to be a part of this world. He was a country boy at heart and he was content to watch the journey of an ant or to lie on his stomach to tickle trout. I felt comfortable too in my kilt and red jumper and fell easily into step with his suggestions for these were the things I also enjoyed. We made love in the heather. There was nothing to mar our first week together. On our last night as we sat alone in the smoking room in front of the log fire, Peter began to talk of serious matters.

"Em, darling," he said, "Remember early on. I asked you what you felt about God and you never told me."

"No," I answered, " because I put it off. I'm not sure in my own mind."

"Well, I want you to know how I think. I won't talk about it again, not unless you ask me. I might think differently in the middle of battle, I don't know. I want to help people, poor people, people who have nothing, people without hope. At the moment, I'm a firm believer in God, the Creator. I've tried to explain this to the chaps but some of them laugh at me so I've shut up. I believe that Christ was the messenger of God. Christ told us to follow the ten commandments and the Church tell us that if we do, we are leading a Christian life. I think we are all servants of God and that it is up to everyone to make the world a better and happier place."

"It sounds easy when you put it like that," I interrupted.

"There are four absolutes that have to be followed," and Peter ticked them off on his fingers as he repeated them, " absolute purity, absolute unselfishness, absolute truth and absolute love."

There was silence between us. "I wish I could say that I lead my life like that, Em, but I do try. I get the mickey taken out of me in the army but it's important to me, especially as I'm set on working overseas when this is all over."

I remained quiet. I didn't know what to say.

"Say something Em," Peter sounded hurt. "I've spoken from my heart. You always go quiet when I want to know what you think."

"I'm sorry, Peter." The words rushed out in my anxiety to give him confidence. "Your thoughts seem so much better ordered than mine. I say my prayers. I go to church but I haven't really thought out what it's all about. Does that make you sad? I try to be kind and thoughtful and I've never knowingly told a lie. I'm glad you don't want to be a priest. I don't think I'd be a good vicar's wife but to go overseas, that would be great."

"That's a long speech, Peter said. "Do you know it's the first time I've heard you express an opinion. When I'm away, I want you to be bold Em, talk to people about the future. Find out what they think will happen when the war is over. Ask them what they think about God and whether they can accept that there are philosophies other than the Christian one." He stood up and looked down at me, his arm resting on the mantelpiece. "And now Emma, my darling..."

"That tone in your voice makes me shudder."

"While we're being serious, there's something else." He bent down and pulled me up beside him. "If I'm ever hurt, you must be brave,"

"Don't Peter, don't, not this week. Not now."

He held me tight and we both stared into the flames. "My pet, it's best talked about. I'm a soldier and I've got to face the war. You've known that from the beginning. I'll be as careful as I can especially now that I have you to come home to. Melville looks after me terribly well and you've no idea what an asset that is. But, my precious, no tears, no looking back, no regrets should I end up as some soldiers do. We've made it. We're together, partners. You'll never be out of my mind. The top part of my thoughts will be on practicalities but you'll be deep in my heart. Should, God willing, you ever give me a son, then I will have more than I could ever dream for, a son by you and me, what a son. Oh, Emmy we have such a future together."

I wept quietly into my arms. I couldn't imagine that such happiness would have to end.

"Come, come," Peter said gently, "I said no tears." He turned me round and we walked slowly up the shallow stairs to our bedroom. We lay on the bed with the big eiderdown pulled over us, too emotionally spent to say any more. I must have slept for, when I woke, Peter was up and about and had run a bath for me.

Melville met us at Crieff. "The captain said it would be O.K.," he reported with a grin. "There's not much call for transport at the weekend. I took your baggage up to your lodgings, fierce landlady. News in France looks a bit dodgy, a bit too quiet for my liking."

Mrs McBride opened the door when we arrived at the lodgings. She was dressed in black from head to foot. A tiny bun of scraped up black hair perched on the top of her head. She was a huge woman with a huge voice.

"Given you my two best rooms," she said by way of introduction. "tea will be at half past five and mind you're not late and I don't know how you expect me to clean the rooms with all these trunks about."

She showed us the rooms. They were both on the first floor. They were spotlessly clean but they were heavily over furnished. An aspidistra blocked out most of the light in the living room and the double bed left little floor space in the bedroom.

"What are we going to do with the luggage?" I asked Melville in despair.

"You sort out what you and the major want and I'll take the rest back to the lines. Plenty of room there."

Tea that evening was a foretaste of what was to come.

"I've done rabbit," Mrs McBride announced. "Can't do more for you till I get your coupons."

We each had a plate piled high with potatoes and cabbage and a few slivers of meat on the side with some dubious looking gravy followed by bread, margarine and peanut butter. We both pretended it was excellent.

"But it's ghastly," I whispered to Peter when the door closed behind her.

"I wish you could do the housekeeping. Perhaps it will be better when she has our coupons. Maybe I could get something from the Mess sergeant. I do wish we could have a place all on our own."

We spent the rest of the day sorting out our luggage and bumping into the furniture. Peter left for work at seven o'clock on the Monday morning ,looking every inch a soldier, boots, rucksack already packed by Melville, camouflaged jacket and an assortment of leather equipment draped across his shoulder.

"Might be late back tonight," he said. "Better tell Mrs McBride I'll eat in the mess, don't want to upset her."

"What about upsetting me?"

"Can't help it Em. It's going to be a lot like this. Try to keep busy. I'll send Melville round about mid-day to collect the luggage we don't need," and with an awkward kiss as the various bits of equipment got in the way, he marched off and I was left alone with the luggage and Mrs McBride. It was not a happy day. When the luggage had gone, I felt adrift, not knowing what to do so I went for a walk. Everyone seemed to stare at me. Nobody spoke. I tried to write some letters but my mood was so glum I didn't want to pass those feelings on.

Peter turned up at half past ten that night, exhausted and dirty.

"I stink like a polecat, must have a bath. Come and talk to me Em. Hope that woman won't disapprove."

The old geyser seemed about to conk out and puffed out steam as well as water. "My, you're filthy. Here, let me scrub your back."

"Damn nuisance, having to lie in ditches and give orders from there. But how's your day been, a bit boring I should think."

"Dead boring," I told him. I wasn't going to tell him how unhappy I had been despite our promises to be honest to each other.

"I was talking to some of the other officers and they said that young women without children or who weren't in reserved occupations..."

"What's that?"

"Oh you know, teaching, nursing, that sort of thing, things that are supposed to be essential, well they're all likely to be called up. Em, I don't want you to be called up. We'd never have our leave at the same time. Do you think you could look for some kind of war work that would save you being conscripted, something temporary, something around here."

"I'll try, I fancy working in a school or on a farm." We talked late into the night. There was so much to say to each other and every minute seemed precious. The church clock struck two. Peter turned and looked at me. "There's one thing we haven't talked about," he said, "and that's the thing that came in the post. Could you use it darling then I won't have to bother and I think it will be nicer for you and you may not feel so dry."

"I'll try, my darling, I'll try," I told him.

I studied the book that told me how to use the nozzle and tubes and puzzled how to use the damn thing. I realised I would have to sit in the bath to use it so I crept across to the bathroom and with poking and prodding I managed to get the thing to work. It was horrid. I couldn't believe I would have to go through that rigmarole every time we made love.

I spent the next few days looking for work and keeping Mrs McBride sweet. Peter was always late for what she called tea and he was always dirty and tired. He always had an excuse but I could see that she was getting fed up.

"You understand all these pressures, Em, so why doesn't the old dragon. We're all keyed up and working like the devil. My men are eager and ready for anything. I can't leave them in the middle of an exercise to arrive on time to eat

Mrs McBride's awful suppers. Still that's enough about me. What about you?"

"I think I've found work. It's on a farm, the Kiplings. They've got a herd of thirty Friesians and I'm to help with the milking and the bottling"

"Sounds great, but can you milk a cow?"

"Course I can't but I can learn. They haven't mentioned money but I don't mind working for nothing as long as I'm not sent away on government work."

The farm was a mile away from Comrie. Mr and Mrs Kipling greeted me warmly. I was given a glass of milk and shown round the farmhouse. Everything seemed to centre round the old black range in the kitchen. Then Mr Kipling took me across to the dairy over a stoned yard that was sticky with mud. He showed me how to massage each teat and how to hold the bucket between my knees while sitting on a three legged stool with my head pressed against the cow's flank. I heard the cow's stomach rumbling when I did this but the animal objected to my attempts to milk it and no milk flowed. I tried to copy what Mr Kipling had showed me. All I got was a whip round the face from the cow's tail.

"Maybe this work ain't for the likes of you," Mr Kipling said and he handed me a bucket of warm soapy water and suggested I washed the udders clean. Then I had to go to the dairy and sterilise the bottles. I then had to cool the warm milk and pour it into the bottles sealing each one with a hand tool. Mr Kipling was a patient teacher and he gave ne two pints of milk each day to take home.

"Mrs McBride will be pleased," I said. "I don't think she likes us very much."

"You don't want to worry about Mrs McBride," Mrs Kipling said with a laugh. "I've known her for years. Her bark's worse than her bite."

A smile spread right across Mrs McBride's face when I presented her with the milk.

During my second week, I was invited to have coffee with the Colonel's wife. She was motherly and pretty. There were other officers' wives there and a number of energetic uncontrolled children. I felt out of place but Mrs Mason took me on one side.

"Emma dear," she said, "this must all seem very strange to you. I hear you've got a job. That's a good idea. Most of the wives here are just visiting. Do remember if you are ever stuck, give me a call. I can generally pull a few strings."

One evening Peter bounced in. "Where are you Emma? I'm on time for once and I've two pieces of news for you. Mother and father have bought a house at Nairn. We'll go and see them when they've settled and... "he paused.

"What's the matter?" I felt the tension in the air.

"The second front has started The allies landed back in France this morning. That's what we've been waiting for. It probably means we won't be here much longer and I don't suppose I'll get across to Nairn with you before I go."

I looked at the floor. I didn't want Peter to see the pain I felt. Then it burst out of me.

"Damn this bloody war. It's mucking up my life."

One afternoon after I had been going to the Kiplings for a month, the farmer arrived home late from the market. He looked tired and harassed. "Perhaps you could get the cows in for me lass. The dogs will help you."

I had never fetched the cows before and I set off with great apprehension. It was a hot afternoon and the bright sun cheered my spirits. The hay was high in the fields and the cows were waiting at the end of the lane.

I opened the gate and the lead cow started to plod up the lane. The dogs rushed round the field chasing out the stragglers. The lead cow was well ahead and, to my horror, I saw her turn into the hayfield. I had forgotten to check that the gates were shut. All the cows had followed her lead and there they were trampling the ready to be mown hay. The cows were becoming bloated with this rich food and I couldn't get them out. I went back to the farm to fetch Mr Kipling. I felt so ashamed.

"I'm really sorry," I said.

"Doing with cows isn't for the likes of you lassie," he said. "Never mind, what's done can't be undone. Come with me and we'll see what we can do together." It looked so easy when Mr Kipling took control.

"I really think I'm more trouble than I'm worth. I think I better look for something in the village. Perhaps it won't be long before..." I stopped in mid sentence. I knew I mustn't mention anything about the battalion moving.

"Just as you like dear," Mrs Kipling said. "I've right enjoyed having you around. Carry on coming until you find something else. Can't stay at McBride's all day. Here have some eggs and extra milk to make you feel better."

I felt better when Mrs McBride showed her pleasure with the extra food and we had fluffy omelettes for tea. Thankfully, Peter was punctual for supper, but afterwards he was quieter than his usual talkative self. He suggested that we went for a walk and we went up to the hills behind the village. We sat on the gate and looked at the view. There were bright colours everywhere.

"It had to come to an end," Peter said urgently. "I knew it had to happen. Now it has and I'm not sure I want it."

"What's happened Pete? What's happened? Tell me."

There was a pause, then he said, "We entrain at Crieff at 6a.m. the day after tomorrow. We march from Comrie. I can't tell you where we're going but I expect you can guess."

I jumped off the gate and stamped my foot. "Damn the war," I shouted, "damn, damn, damn."

"You can always stay with Mother and Father," Peter said. "I know they'll look after you."

I looked at Peter's haggard face. "Cheer up love. You've got what you wanted." As soon as I had uttered the words I knew I had hurt him. We stood there not knowing what to say to each other and then we were in each others arms and we were talking. By the time I had finished telling him about the disaster with the cows, we were both laughing. We walked back arm in arm. We spent most of the night sorting things out. We decided to give Mrs McBride a week's notice and I would tell the Kiplings that I was leaving the village.

The village seemed to hum the next day. Nobody mentioned the imminent departure of the battalion. Women flitted from shop to shop tight faced and serious. When I told the Kiplings I was leaving, they said," Aye and we'll be a bit sad in this house tonight. You have given us old folks a wee bit of pleasure." She put some cheese and more eggs into my bicycle basket. The two kindly people stood at the gate and waved until I had turned the corner. In the afternoon, I looked out Melville.

"I've come to thank you for all you've done. Look after the major for me and good luck to you both."

"Thankyou Ma'am," he said. "The major will look after me and I'll look after him. Here's a wee thing to bring you luck," and he handed me a sprig of white heather. He saluted as I cycled off.

The love that flowed between us was passionate and prolonged that night. Peter was a keyed up young officer and I was a tense young wife. We were both anxious about what the future would bring. The love making for me was only spoilt by the session in the bath with the complicated tubing and nozzle. Peter could only have slept for two hours before I heard him creeping about in the bedroom.

"I was hoping you wouldn't hear me, darling," he said as I stirred. "Last night was so prefect that I want to leave you with those memories. Now we'll just have to pretend to be brave. Shut your eyes, Emma. Don't look, don't move. I'm going to slip away."

I lay there frozen with shock and panic, unable to move. I didn't want that minute to be happening. I heard his boots crunching on the pavement. After a while, I shook myself. I couldn't let him leave like that. I dressed myself and slipped out of the house. It was four o'clock. I walked down to the churchyard thinking all the time of the occasions that I had walked that way with Peter on my arm.

There was a heavy grey mist covering the village and moisture from the trees dripped coldly down on me as I waited. Then I heard the faint skirl of the pipes and steadily the sound drew nearer. Nearer and nearer they came and I heard the added sound of marching boots and through the mist came the piper looking so proud and magnificent. Curtains were drawn back from windows as others watched the men leaving. Then I saw Peter, ahead of his beloved men, tall and confident. Crunch, crunch, crunch, hundreds of boots marched in unison. I didn't want Peter to see me and I sheltered behind a tombstone. Company after company marched by, eyes front, arms swinging, packs swaying. Then the sound of the pipes started to grow fainter and it was as if they were drawing my soul into their sound. The mist lay its mantle of silence and curtains dropped back into place. I felt part of me was marching with Peter and I didn't want him to go. Slowly I walked back to our room, cold with the mist and fog but colder still with the sense of foreboding that filled my body.

I lit the small gas fire and tried to rub some warmth into my fingers. I wanted to pray but I couldn't find the words. I had to pull myself together. I had to find some purpose in my life. I started to tidy the two rooms but everything I touched brought back a memory.

"A taxi's coming for me at twelve o'clock Mrs McBride. It's best that I go and stay with Peter's parents. We've squared up for the week so that's alright isn't it?"

Mrs McBride's large figure filled the doorway. She seemed to want to linger. Then, with a sigh, she muttered, "Och aye," and turned away. She returned a few minutes later with a parcel of sandwiches. "For your lunch," she said. "Sure I'll be missing you both. I'll call when the taxi comes."

I had arranged for Peter's heavy gear to be sent to Nairn. I took as much as possible with me booking it through in the goods van at Edinburgh. It was a difficult morning tinged with loneliness. I felt I would scream if I had to deal with any more boxes. I hadn't unpacked some of the things I had brought from Shillong.

The Whites greeted me warmly. They wanted to know all about Peter but there was little I could tell them.

"He left with his battalion this morning and I presume he'll go to France but I don't know. I don't know when I shall see him again."

"Now don't fret Emma," Sir Aubrey tucked my arm in his. "You can stay here as long as you like but come and see the house. I hope you'll like it."

"There's still a lot to do dear, but you can help," Lady Olivia added. I saw familiar shaped packing cases and boxes and pictures stacked in the corner.

The house seemed to go on for ever and our footsteps echoed on the carpetless floors. The kitchen alone was bigger than the two rooms we had rented at Mrs McBride's. The house seemed lifeless and gloomy and I wondered how two elderly people could fill such a place with warmth and humanity.

We sat in the living room with trays on our knees. A wood fire crackled in the grate although it was a warm summer's day. We sat in big leather chairs and half filled book cases lined the walls. I looked out on the wilderness of the garden. Sir Aubrey saw me looking and started to talk about all the things that needed doing, new beds to be laid, trees to be pruned.

Lady Olivia showed me a list of things that needed to be done. "There's more yet," she added. "I'm only just beginning to get things shipshape."

My heart sank as I realised she expected me to stay and help. I didn't want to stay too long. I needed independence and work, something to occupy my mind.

"You know, Peter wants me to get a job, something where I would have accommodation and where I would be free to move about so that I could meet up with him when he has leave. Have you any ideas?"

"I have," Lady Olivia replied. "We were talking about it in town. Hospitals want people to help with amenities, paid or unpaid. There are so many young soldiers arriving back in England. I've a friend in the Red Cross in Edinburgh. They're always looking for people to help. I'll get in touch with her."

"Well done, dear," Sir Aubrey said. "you always seem to know someone somewhere."

"That would be great if you would. I'll help while I'm here but I'd like to get settled as soon as possible."

Lady Olivia spent a lot of time phoning Edinburgh. Her efforts resulted in the offer of a job.

"They want you to work in a big hospital on the Glasgow Road," she told me. "It's near Bathgate. You'll be helping the almoner. It used to be a lunatic asylum but part of it is empty and waiting for any war wounded. The other part is occupied by elderly people that have been evacuated from London. They'll tell you what you have to do when you get there. All I know is that you'll have officer status and you'll be expected to wear a uniform."

"That sounds great. Thankyou very much."

"I've got to let headquarters know when you're ready to start. They're taking you on my recommendation. I've explained all about Peter."

"I'm surprised they don't want to interview me."

"It's a case of who they can get these days," Lady Olivia said tactlessly.

"When would you like to go?" Sir Aubrey asked. "We'd like you to stay for ever but it's best to go."

"Perhaps I can stay for a week. Peter might have phoned by then and it will give them time to get ready for me."

And Peter phoned the following morning. "Darling, darling, are you alright? Yes, I know you're at Nairn. Look Em, let me do the talking. We're still in England. Gosh I've got to be careful what I say. We have to stay in camp all the time and all our letters are censored. You've got work, splendid. Let me have the address. We're only allowed one phone call a week. The men are bored to bits and we have to keep them occupied. I'm doing the boxing. Em, sorry for the talk but I wrote down everything I wanted to say. Damn. There's the pips. Darling, I love..... "

"Yes, that was Peter," I told the Whites who were waiting anxiously beside me. "They're still in England. It was lovely to hear him but he sounded so strange, so detached."

That night in bed, I tried to recall every word he had said. I felt so lonely. Sir Aubrey was kind and gentle. Lady Olivia was always so busy. The next morning, I sat down and wrote to Di. I told her everything. A reply came by return.

Dearest Emma

I'm so pleased you have written and I have an address for you. I've an enormous piece of news. Daddy is back. Can you believe it? He was smuggled out across the south of France and through Spain. He's so thin and he doesn't look like Daddy. I'm a bit frightened of him. He walks about at night dressed in a towel. He can't sleep and he has terrible dreams. Mum is wonderful. She never pushes him, just sees to everything he wants. She's so happy to have him home.

I still work in the city but it's hard with these doodlebugs, never know where they're going to land.. One cut out as I was coming out of the tube. You should have seen me scuttle back. We hate them worse than the bombing.

So you're on your own again, poor old Emma. Fancy milking or not milking the cows, can't imagine you doing that. You've had so many jobs and here I am stuck in the same old one.

We should love to see you again, don't forget to bring your ration card. Every little bit helps as the monkey said when he spat in the teapot (quote from Granny). Think of us nursing Dad back to normality and we'll think of you missing Peter. I'm so glad I met him. I went dancing last weekend with another man. He was awful, kept telling me how much money he made before he was called up.

What do you think of this envelope. Mum spends hours making them. They're almost impossible to buy,

Do try and visit us, best love from your old school pal,

Di

I felt better for reading Di's letter but began to worry about the doodlebugs and wondered how Aunt Mathilda was coping as I settled down to another round of unpacking and sorting.

The Whites took me to the station. I wore my new and only suit. I felt I had to make a good impression. The in-laws seemed in low spirits.

"We've enjoyed having you, Emma," Lady Olivia said.

"We'll miss you. Be sure to give us all the news of Pater. Reverse the charges if it's easier. Don't worry about us. We've got Vivienne coming up soon with the children. That'll liven us up. Visit us whenever you feel like it. We can help each other along," and Sir Aubrey gave me a wink.

"I shouted my goodbyes as the train chugged out of the station. I wasn't sad at saying goodbye but every goodbye meant a journey into the unknown.. I settled down with the paper but what I read depressed me. There were reports of severe casualties along the front There were heavy onslaughts with women and children being caught in the crossfire. Reinforcements were necessary. Churches had been bombed and schools were being used as barracks. I couldn't go on. It all seemed so real now that somebody close to me was involved.

I left my luggage at the station and made my way to the Red Cross office off Princes Street. I felt the war had bypassed Edinburgh as I passed the well stocked shops. The Commandant was an awesome, red haired lady. She took me under her wing and explained what some of my duties would be.

"You won't be getting a big salary but then you can feel free to do as you like with Matron's permission of course. Your hours are flexible and they've found you a room in the nurses' wing. That's all I can tell you. Matron will fill in the details."

This information was fed to me as I was trying on the Red Cross navy uniform, Fortunately there was a large jacket that matched a smaller waisted skirt.

"You're lucky," the girl said as she bundled the clothes into a bag. "They're second hand so you won't need coupons. I can let you have some of these shirts and ties too and you'll need a peaked cap but you must have a pair of black shoes. Have you coupons for those?"

"Yes, I'll get some this afternoon."

I paid an incredibly small amount for the clothes and then set off to buy my shoes and make my way to the station forecourt for six o'clock. I stood and watched the people and buses and carts moving slowly about their business. No-one seemed to hurry. A small car drew up.

"You must be Emma. Put your luggage in the back and hop in," another lady in a navy blue uniform was at the wheel.

"I hope you enjoy it dear," she said as we drove along. "It's twelve miles out and there's only two buses a day so you'll have to plan your day off. It's a bit quiet at the moment but that'll change when the casualties start coming in," she drove up to a sombre, Victorian building. A young nurse came to the door when I rang.

"I'm to take you straight to the nurses' home," she said. There was no welcome in her voice. "Is this your luggage? You've got enough for an army." I tried to thank the Red Cross driver but she drove off at speed and I was left to follow the unfriendly nurse. She lead me up staircase after staircase to a small room under the eaves.

"Supper's at seven," she said. "Water's hot most of the time and the telephone's on the ground floor. Hope you don't get many calls. It's too far to come and fetch you. Washing and ironing in the basement. I want to get off duty so, if there's nothing else you need, I'll be off," and she was gone before I had time to utter a word.

The room appeared as unfriendly as the nurse. It was tiny. There was a small cupboard, a chair and an iron bedstead. It was already cold although it was summer and I couldn't see any form of heating. I was too nervous and unhappy to go for supper and waited hungrily for breakfast. The dining room was cafeteria service so that presented no problems. I drank strong tea and ate fresh baps, putting one in my pocket for later on in case I missed another meal.

At 8.45. I waited outside Matron's office. It smelt of polish and disinfectant. Matron was a small woman with bright blue eyes. "Well Emma," she said, "we're very short of someone to look after what I call amenities. We've a lot of old people who have been evacuated from the south and they have visitors who need to be shown around and told where they can find accommodation. Some of the patients need shopping done for them and when the soldiers come there'll be a lot to do. It's the kind of job that grows on you but I'm sure you'll cope very well." Matron's warmth made me feel welcome.

"What are my hours and how much will I be paid?"

"You won't have set hours and you'll be paid two pounds ten shillings a week all found. You have one day off a week but let me know when your husband is off duty and we'll see what we can fix up. Now Maria will look after you."

I walked along to Maria's office but that was empty so I found my way up to the old people's ward and started my first visit. That night, after a stodgy supper, I sat down and wrote to Peter.

Darling Peter,

This is my second night here. This hospital is an old Victorian shambles. It used to be a loony bin but most of the loonies have gone goodness knows where. Some of the wards are full of old and senile people from London, thirty of forty in a ward in rows on each side. They look at me grinning without teeth. When I speak to them most of them just laugh. They don't reply. They just lay there day after day. Are they being kept alive just for the sake of it? The nurses are running all the time. They make me feel in the way, the same as they do in the nurses' home. They scarcely talk to me. My uniform is a navy blue suit with a bus conductor's hat. I feel a banana in it. My room is at the top of the building and it's even smaller than the one we had at Mrs McBride's. I've had one bath and it was cold. There now. that's a list of my moans. You're probably sleeping on the floor and washing from a canvas basin. I'll be more cheerful in my next letter. I get one day off a week and I have to let them know when you are free.

The old folks were a bit sad when I left them but they're looking forward to Viv's visit. It's a barn of a house, much too big for them. I adore your Dad. You're right. He's a smasher. Just like his son. You'll have to call me at the office. The nurses won't call me down from the top floor. I'll stay late if I know when you're going to phone.

I can't write lovey dovey things, I feel too uptight but, in spite of everything, you are my own man who I worship,

A rotten letter from your Emmy.

I decided to go to Edinburgh on my first day off. I planned to look at the shops and go to a matinee but I did wish I had someone to go with. I waited at the bus stop. I was early because I didn't know how punctual the buses were. A lorry pulled up in front of me and the driver peered down from his cab and asked if I would like a lift.

"Yes please," I said and, lifting my tight skirt, I clambered up into the cab. "Anywhere near Princes Street would be fine."

The driver did not answer. He was a middle aged man with tattooed arms. As we approached the centre of the city, I said innocently, "Anywhere here please."

"That's what you might want but it's not what I want," he said, his mouth hardening into a sneer. I began to feel frightened.

"Put me down, please, just anywhere. Just here. We're well past Princes Street."

"You're a bit green aren't yer, thinking I'd put you down like that. Nice bit of fluff you look to me."

"Put me down at once," I was frightened and angry.

The driver slipped his greasy hand up my thigh. I tried to get as much space as I could between us.

"Not on yer nellie, you're coming wiv me." The driver was moving slowly through the traffic but the cab was so high that the people alongside us couldn't see what was happening. He had to slow down at a red light so, seizing the opportunity, I opened the door and jumped, my hat and handbag went flying. Nobody attempted to help me instead they started to hoot to hurry me out of the way. I picked up my things and with as much dignity that I could muster, I stalked to the pavement. I looked back at the lorry. The driver was sitting there laughing. I had a lot to learn. I headed towards Princes Street and a cup of coffee, trying hard to calm myself and vowing that I wouldn't tell Peter.

I tried to get familiar with the work over the next few weeks. My legs and feet were tired with walking along the endless corridors. I admired the nurses who worked far harder than I did but never seemed to complain. I hardly saw Maria, my supervisor. She was busily occupied flirting with a Polish officer. She seemed to be pleased that I was there if only to have more time with him. I envied her.

Matron called me one day and told me that she wanted me to take the relatives of patients who had died to view the bodies so that they could identify them. "Remember that it will be an emotional experience for them and that they will be tired. Most of them will have travelled overnight but it's a job that has to be done."

It was a week later that the next patient died. I lead a tired and bedraggled group to the mortuary. The place was cold and damp and there was only a single greenish bulb to light the whole length of the room. I had been told that it was the third body on the left. There was a line of white clothed corpses, each had a right foot protruding and a luggage label was tied to the big toe. I walked to the third body trying not to feel the aura and smell of death that pervaded the whole place. Slowly I turned the sheet back revealing a green face with sunken eyes and gaping mouth. Nothing had been done to the body since the patient had died. The visitors took one look and burst into tears. "That's Gran," said a white haired lady, wiping her nose. "Look at her eyebrows. Oh, poor darling, left lying there all on her own. The two men tut tutted and looked ashamed of their tears. I lead the group across to the almoner who dealt kindly with the mechanics of death and burial.

The experience shook me up. I went and bought a bun and ate it in the grounds. I couldn't face any more elderly people, not then. I didn't feel that I had dealt with the people sympathetically. I hadn't known what to say. I'd never had any experience of death. I would have liked to talk to someone about it, I went back to the office and Maria was there but her only interest in life was her Polish boyfriend and she couldn't talk about anything else. If only I could share these moments with Peter.

I spent the evening in my little room. I wished I had a friend to whom I could talk but at least I had the time to write letters. I wrote to Peter every day, telling him everything that happened. I tried to keep my letters cheerful and hide the loneliness that dogged me. Peter wrote to me twice a week and they were my lifeline. His letters arrived out of chronological order and some of them worried me.

Emmy. my precious,

We're still here. I'm getting frantic. The officers are getting edgy and the men impatient. Why can't we get a move on. We're missing it all. We've trained so long and now it's difficult to keep up the men's morale now that we're confined to this wretched camp. No visits from anyone and a weekend's leave once a month. I gave mine up to an officer whose wife had just had a baby. I run the boxing and we do lots of training sessions but that only helps a few lads but why am I ranting on like this? Your wonderful letters continue to arrive. They keep me in balance, but Emmy darling, what really is happening? I can sense that you're lonely but you never say so. I've a sneaky feeling I know why. Write me the good and the bad darling, we did promise didn't we? I want a proper picture of how you are. And I would like a studio photo of you, a large one and a small one. I'll carry the small one in my breast pocket and peep at it from time to time. I've only the little one we took when we were picnicking at Shillong, remember?

I'm very well, very keyed up but another side of me misses you dreadfully. I didn't think I would ever feel like this. I have a lot to learn,

Your adoring Peter.

The day after this letter was more difficult than usual. There was a note on my desk saying that there was a man on ward 14 who was anxious about his money affairs and wanted to write a letter to his wife. The nurses found it difficult to understand him although he was very intelligent but he had cancer of the mouth and they didn't have much time to spend with him. I spent the afternoon with him and wrote to Peter that evening.

My loving Man,

Your letter came this morning in which you told me to write honestly. Well, I need to as I'm rather upset. I had to visit a man who had cancer of his mouth, throat and tongue. I had to help him write a letter to his wife about money matters. Peter, it was horrible. Great ropes of phlegm were hanging down the back of his throat. He had no teeth, lips or tongue and he smelt. I could hardly bear to look at him. I had to get quite close to him to hear the funny noises he was making. I tried to look him straight in the eyes but I could see that he knew how I was feeling. He'd a wonderful, pleading stare. How do the nurses cope with him day after day? They never seem to turn a hair and here I am all gone to pieces after a couple of hours with him. I fixed up some sort of letter for him and he squeezed my hand. I think he had forgotten that he had no lips to kiss me with. I've had two more buns to calm me down. I find they help. I feel I want to wash myself from top to toe. This is one of the worst cases I've had to see to but there are many others, not as bad as this man.

You say you have a lot to learn. That makes two of us. In spite of all my travels, I'm so ignorant. Wish we could do our learning together. You seem fraught, a lesson in patience to be learned?

I can't say I'm unhappy, just in a state of constant bewilderment. I'm rather isolated here, the others all have their own cliques and I can't find a slot. There's no way of meeting the locals except for a chance meeting on the bus. Perhaps it will be more lively when the military comes. Has this letter upset you? It's certainly helped me to write it. I don't feel quite so alone. Don't go giving your weekends away too often. The baby in my make-up needs your support,

From your loving Emma.

It was a Wednesday afternoon in early September that Peter phoned.

"Darling I've got the weekend at last, from 8 o'clock on Saturday morning until 6pm on Sunday. I'll be at Kings Cross as soon as I can after eight. I'll meet you there. I'll fix a hotel. Isn't it wonderful. I won't take no for an answer. There's a great queue for the phone, everybody fixing things up. Must fly. Love you and I'll tell you that on Saturday." The phone clicked and I hadn't said a word.

I went into action quickly. The first thing was to get matron's permission. I planned to travel down on Friday night and back on Sunday night in time for work on Monday. My tummy churned with excitement.

I chose my clothes carefully. I wanted Peter to be proud of me. I left the hospital at four o'clock and treated myself to supper in Edinburgh. I took care to arrive half an hour early for the 10 o'clock train. I wanted to make sure of a seat but there wasn't one to be had not in third class. There were plenty of empty ones in the first. I stood in the corridor and, as soon as the train started, I sat on my small case.

"That's not much of a seat," laughed a soldier who had wedged his rucksack into a corner and was perched on that

"Too right," I said wryly.

He rolled up his greatcoat. "You better have this, "he said. "Your legs will swell if you stand all the way to London. It'll take eight hours."

It was more comfortable with the coat. I wished I'd worn my uniform, then I could have had a seat in first class. By the time we arrived at Kings Cross, my mouth was dry and tasted of soot. It was too early for Peter, so I had a wash and brush up and a cup of coffee and put the horrors of the journey behind me. I waited by the entrance to the underground and then he was there. I flung my arms round his neck, quite forgetting he was an officer and didn't like displays of affection in public.

"Let's get a taxi," he said, "then I can tell you how I feel."

We didn't talk much in the taxi. It was enough to be together. We stayed at the same hotel where the Whites had lived and were shown to a suite of rooms on the first floor.

"Now I've got you, I don't know what to say," Peter was grinning. "Come on Emmie, lie with me. Let me feel you. I might be able to unwind with you in my arms."

"Peter, I haven't brought that thing with me with the tubes. Can you manage?"

"Yes, pet, yes. Just lie with me. My head's going round and round. I can't believe I'm with you. It's been so long, it feels like an eternity."

Slowly, I undid his buttons and released his prickly battle dress. Slowly I undid his trousers. Slowly and with exquisite tenderness we made love. We lay on the bed all morning, drowsy, loving, drawing together, drowning the pressures of the yesterdays.

Suddenly Peter said, "My God I'm hungry. Shall we paint the town red. Let's go to the theatre and have dinner afterwards but now we'll have lunch and dawdle through the park."

We went downstairs to the restaurant and had lunch, then for the rest of the weekend, we did everything we wanted regardless of the expense. We rose to the heights of euphoria that we had never experienced before. I watched the play at the theatre but have no memory of it. I ate a beautifully served meal but porridge would have tasted just as good. We were basking in being together. The weekend was so short that it made every minute important, precious. But, in spite of our happiness, there were the tensions of war pressing down on us. We walked back across St James Park in the twilight of the summer evening. It had been a gloriously summer's day. We were at Waterloo at four o'clock on the Sunday afternoon for the Southampton train. The platform was crowded with servicemen and their families.

"Well at least I know where you'll be," I joked. "It's written on the side of the train," but the joke fell flat. Peter was inside himself once more, the disciplined officer.

"Emmy darling, I want you to go now, none of this staying till the last minute. I don't think I could control myself. Please go, Em." Peter took off his glengarrie and kissed me on the lips. There was no passionate hug, no tender words. They had all been said in the hotel. Then he covered his head, saluted me and, picking up his gear, marched off. I looked at the people around me and saw the different ways the families were dealing with their emotions. I was glad that Peter had left quickly but wished the pounding of my heart would stop. I went to the toilet and sobbed, pulling the chain from time to time to hide the sounds.

Then I pulled myself together. I decided I could have time to get across to Hurlingham to see Di if I got a move on. I rinsed my face and made my way across the platform averting my gaze from the women leaving the Southampton platform.

"Come in, come in," Mrs Turnball greeted me. "have you got Peter with you? Now look who we have here," and she lead me through to the sitting room. I had to take a deep breath to hide my shock. Mr Turnball had changed from the big, physical man he had been to a bent, grey haired skeleton but the dark eyes were just the same, piercing yet laughing.

"Well now, this is fine," he said rising to his feet. "Come and sit down here and tell me everything." He must have noticed the look on my face because he added, "Don't worry child, with these two women looking after me, I'll soon be as right as rain."

Mrs Turnball brought in some tea and carrot cake. "It's the best I can do," she said. "Even with Arthur's extra rations I find it hard to eke things out."

I had to tell them about Peter. "Actually," I said, "we've just had a night together and I don't know when....." I had to stop talking because my voice sounded knotted. We talked of other things until it was time to leave. Di walked with me to the underground station.

"He never talks about it," she said. "Sometimes we wish he would talk. It might help him but he's better than he was. Mum's wonderful with him and Emm." she stopped talking and looked at me.

"Go on," I said.

"I think I've found someone I really like. Can't mention it to anyone yet."

"I won't tell a soul, " I promised, " and Di, you can keep my secret. The hospital's bloody awful and I hate it. It's done me good to come and see you. It's put things into perspective. I mustn't feel sorry for myself."

When I reached Kings Cross I found a carriage marked "Ladies only" on the Edinburgh night train. It was empty and I thought I would have a chance to put my legs up. The whistle blew and I started to sort myself out when the door was thrown open and eight young American G.I.s tumbled in.

"Hey buddy, that sure was a close run thing," a brawny, close cropped young man laughed.

"Did you know this compartment is ladies only?" I asked him.

"That's why it's so empty," "and I've never seen anyone less like ladies than you lot."

"You going to shove us off?"

"No, I don't mind but I'm not overkeen on smoking."

The newcomers relaxed and started arranging their luggage. One took his rucksack into the corridor and started fiddling with his tin opener and an assortment of tins. Another produced canned drinks. Before long, we were sitting squashed together laughing and talking and enjoying a picnic of the kind of food I hadn't seen since I had arrived in England. The heat of the carriage began to make me feel sleepy.

"I'm so glad you made this carriage," I said," but I must try and get some sleep. I've got to work in the morning." I explained that I had just seen my husband off to war and they were even more solicitous. One made a pillow for me, another pushed up so that I could put my feet on the opposite seat and another covered me with his coat.

"You make me feel like a blooming queen," I laughed, "but thanks for everything."

The G.I.s woke me as we approached Edinburgh.

"If I had a home, I'd ask you all round for a drink but have a good time in England."

I was well into the hospital routine again by the end of the week when I received a buff envelope containing a terse note informing me that Peter had gone overseas and giving me a different field Post Office address for him. Part of me was pleased that he had got into battle at last and part of me hated the thought. The pictures in the papers were horrible. We were advancing but at what a cost. I thought of Peter in those scenes and wondered how he would cope. How would he manage sleeping in a ditch, wet and cold? What would he feel like if he had to shoot someone? It was strange how personalised it had all become.

Casualties had started to arrive in the empty wards, young men wounded, some blinded, some too shocked to discuss their experiences. One afternoon I arrived at the biggest casualty ward when a voice called out, "Ere Miss." a young man with half a leg strung up at an angle tried to catch my eye. "Have you got time to talk to Rusty? 'e can 'ear us 'cos 'e does what 'e's told but 'e won't smile or say anyfing. You 'ave a go with 'im, Miss."

I sat on Rusty's bed. True to his name he had carrot coloured hair and the palest of blue eyes. He looked at me unblinking and unsmiling. I wasn't sure how to begin.

"Nice to see you, Rusty," I began. "I come round each day to see if I can do anything for you. Would you like me to write a letter?"

Silence.

"It's nice and quiet here. Are any of your pals here?"

Silence.

"Are you in a Scottish regiment? My husband is."

Silence.

"Look, I'll pop round and see you tomorrow." I reached out and squeezed his hand. It fell back on the bed when I released it.

"See you tomorrow, Rusty."

"He's like that all the time," a young soldier called out, "but the Doc says he'll be alright. Did you say your husband's in a Scottish regiment? That makes you one of us," and he pointed to his tam o' shanter hanging on the end of his bed. "Had it hard we did but we did alright."

A tight feeling came into my throat that stopped me asking any questions. That night I wrote to Peter.

My darling,

There's been no letter from you. I hope mine have arrived. I address them to this new .F.P.O. number. The wounded are coming in now to the wards and they mentioned the number of your division. I tried not to show any emotion. All this training in the hills and now you're amongst all these dykes and flatness. Several of the lads are from regiments this side of the border. I don't feel lonely any more. Can you believe that. Even the nurses are talking to me and of course, with the old people as well as the military, I'm getting busier and busier. I'm getting quite good at sorting out problems and the mothers of the soldiers are so grateful for any help. Some of the young wives are a bit weepy. I'm in constant touch with Nairn. Viv is there with the children. I have a sneaking feeling that they're very naughty. Perhaps I'll do better one day.

One of the ex residents is a real loony. He's been kept on as a cleaner and he's very odd. When there's a full moon, he spends the whole week cleaning one step in the hall, over and over again. All you can see is his large bottom sticking up,. At least he's unaware of all the unhappiness going on around him.

Sometimes I feel it will be a million years before I see you again. Sometimes I feel a million years old. I think it's my bad time of the month, always feel a bit depressed then.

Is there anything you need. Do you manage to keep your feet clean? Oh, there's so much I want to know but there's one thing that's certain. You give me meaning to my life. Take care.

Your loving WIFE - Emm

Three weeks later the allies were thrusting through Belgium and Holland. I was sitting at my desk when matron came in.

"Hello dear," she said, "are you getting along alright?"

"Yes, thankyou, Matron."

Then I saw the orange envelope in her hand.

"What is it Matron? Tell me. It's news of Peter isn't it? Tell me quickly."

"It's nothing bad, dear. Look," and she passed the telegram to me. "You must know that I always open telegrams when they come to the hospital," but I wasn't listening. I was reading the telegram slowly.

"War Office regret to inform you that Major White was slightly wounded on September 25th stop. He will be returned to U.K. soonest possible stop Will notify you details of hospital stop."

"Don't worry too much, dear," Matron's usually smiling face was solemn. She fidgeted with her cap.

"You must wait until you hear which hospital he's in, then you can go straight there. Must make the most of our young men these days," and she turned to go but she stopped at the door. "Just sit for a while and let me know if there's anything I can do."

My mind was in a turmoil. I sat there wondering what slightly wounded meant. I wondered if the lad with half a leg was considered slightly wounded. I wondered if Peter was in pain and how long it would be before I saw him. I decided to phone Sir Aubrey and reverse the charges. I hoped he would answer and not Lady Olivia. I couldn't face going round the wards. I felt too tearful and I was too worried.

I managed to clear the letters on my desk and was starting to clear up when the phone rang. It was the almoner to tell me that Peter had been admitted to a hospital in Derby along with other members of his battalion. He had been admitted that morning but was not in pain. She asked me to visit at the weekend. I phoned Nairn again. I felt relieved to know he was back in England. At least he was in a warm, clean bed. I told Matron's secretary that I planned to leave on Friday night and would be back on Sunday evening. I ate a little supper but I wasn't hungry. Even the nurses were solicitous and one of them brought a cup of cocoa to my room.

Once again, I arrived at the station early and was lucky enough to find a corner seat in a carriage that did have a corridor and a toilet. I did sleep a little but when I arrived at Derby, my feet were sore and swollen. I booked a room at The Station Hotel and asked the receptionist the way to the hospital explaining that my husband had arrived there from the front. Her attitude changed immediately and even suggested that she would keep the evening meal for me if I was late. The hospital was only a short walk away. It was when I reached the reception desk at the hospital that the nerves started. I could hardly move one foot in front of the other. I was directed along high ceilinged corridors with wards on either side where I could see men either lying or sitting beside their beds. It smelt of ether and disinfectant. When I reached Peter's ward, I stood in the doorway and looked. There were men with arms and legs strung in odd positions, some with cages over their legs, some with bandages round their heads. I saw scenes like this every day in my own hospital and didn't get nervous there but this was different. My man was here and he was suffering..

"Major White?" I asked at the sister's desk.

"Second bed from the end on the left."

Catcalls followed me as I walked down the ward looking for Peter's bed. I waved back. Peter spotted me first and called out. I rushed towards him and hugged him regardless of the crescendo of whistles.

"Don't fret, Emm. It's a clean wound. Bullet in and out the top of the thigh. Once the bleeding had stopped, it was fine. Now it's got to heal, but I expect you can guess..."

"I know, sick as a dog you're not there, but I'm glad you're not."

"We took it bad. Three of my officers were killed and I think eighteen men. Can't find out the facts yet. Some of the men are here. Melville was wonderful, made sure I was all trussed up. Em, can you look out for the others if they come to your hospital. I feel I've let them all down. It was a sniper that got me. We were in an orchard studying a map and ping. I'm still worked up. Forgive me. I'm going to try and get out of this place this afternoon with crutches. Then we can go somewhere and talk but I must have a pair of shoes. I can't clump round in these boots."

"I'll go and buy some this morning. Give me something to do."

I collected a shopping list from Peter's fellow patients. There was an air of tension in the ward and many of the men had dark patches underneath their eyes.

"I'll be back about two," I told Peter, "and we can get a taxi to the hotel."

I struggled round the strange city looking for their requirements. Envelopes were hard to find, cigarettes had to be queued for, and size 12 shoes were very difficult to track down. Footsore, but with a completed shopping list, I returned to the ward and handed over the purchases. Everyone was delighted, but most of them had no money on them and were covered with embarrassment when they realised this. I made a joke of it and said it was all part of my war work; I hoped Peter was proud of me. I was sad their relatives had been unable to reach these men, perhaps with families it was not easy to arrange an instant visit.

When I returned Peter was dressed and practising on his crutches. It was easier with the firm footing of the new shoes which proved a perfect fit. He looked incongruous with his dirty uniform and brand new shoes. We caught a taxi to the hotel, and took a lift up to the grotty bedroom. It seemed like heaven. We didn't notice the colour, the smell, the thin net curtains. I lay him on the bed with my coat over his legs, and I sat in a chair beside him. Then Peter started to tell me of the awfulness of war. I tried to stop him. I wasn't feeling emotionally strong enough to hear the details. Soon he dropped off in a doze and I pulled my chair close and lay my head by his on the pillow. It was uncomfortable but after the squashed up train ride I fell asleep. It was tea-time when we both woke, so I explored the gloomy place to see if they would allow us a tray of tea. Smiling and eager to help the receptionist said she would do her best and a tray soon appeared with two grubby cups and saucers, a little milk and tea so weak it took more like water. We decided it would be better if Peter went back to the hospital for his supper and an early night. He was clearly not strong. I had supper in the dingy dining room.

Sunday was better, we enjoyed a hot lunch in the hotel. In the afternoon, Peter hobbled into a nearby park. By now we were laughing and happy.

I had a chat with Sister before I left. "The wounds are already showing signs of healing. He's doing very well, but I think we should keep him here another week. Then he must ask for a month's leave before he returns to duty." Off she bustled. With so many in her charge she had no time for small talk.

"Must phone Nairn," Peter insisted. They'll have us, I'm sure. It's a damn nuisance though. Battles are hotting up more and more, and here I am, stuck…"

"But what about me?" I asked nettled and really hurt. "Don't you think a month with me would be rather nice."

"Darling, darling, don't take on so. It isn't that I don't want to be with you. Surely you understand. For years I've trained myself and been trained to fight, and now I'm out of it with a small wound. A thousand years with you would be lovely… but… Oh Hell, I'm all mixed up. Don't press me Emma, just go on loving me."

"I'll never stop that, and I'm going to make the most of every moment. Wish we'd a place of our own to go to. I know mother will boss me around and do things for you that I want to do." With a considerable amount of standing still at the public phone, Peter got through to his father, who was delighted. He gave us an open invitation to visit them whenever it was needed.

"It's best at Nairn," Peter sat down suddenly on the bed, he looked blue with fatigue. "They'll know a local doctor, and we'll be able to help them. And I'll be able to see Viv, it's ages since I've seen her."

"Heavens, I'd forgotten they were there too. That's the whole family of Whites and just me. I'll have to be on my best behaviour and not mind…"

"What I suggest," Peter interrupted, he seemed almost too tired to talk, "is that they put me on a train here, and we join up in Edinburgh. I don't think there'll be much walking, all trains come and go from the same level. You'll fix up the Edinburgh to Nairn bit, won't you, and get the Matron's permission."

He shut his eyes.

I'll do everything, but I think I'd better go now. Your'e absolutely dished. Let me know dates and your trains. Good-bye for a week, Peter, only a week." I kissed him on his closed eyelids, and he mumbled something under his breath.

I caught the night train back to Edinburgh which was already full up and late to arrive. I searched up and down the train, but could find no seat, so had to settle for a space in the corridor. I sat on the floor, the draught whistled round my kidneys. My coat wasn't big enough to cover all of me and those bits exposed to the cold became numb. Occasionally I dozed, only to be woken when the train stopped at a station and someone climbed over me. It seemed an endless night, and on arrival my feet were again swollen and my legs were stiff. I viewed the oncoming day's work with apprehension, two restless nights out of three made me stiff and dull in my head.

The following week flew by. I had permission from Matron to stay away as long as was necessary and I checked the trains to Nairn. I also managed to track down three soldiers from Peter's battalion, all in the same ward.

This was now full to bursting point, the nurses walked at top speed from one to another carrying dressings and medicines. All of the soldiers described the heavy fighting, the mud, the noise, the empty streets and the shell-like buildings. The effect of wounded children, lying doll like in the gutter hurt them most badly. All three were glad to be out of it, fortunately only one was seriously hurt. They were married men with and could count on time together. I wished Peter would feel like that.

The meeting in Edinburgh with Peter on his crutches and the journey to Nairn went without a hitch. Luggage was no problem, Peter had none. We travelled first class and there was room for Peter to straighten his leg. The house was big enough to accommodate us all, including Viv's two boisterous children and a young nanny. I felt swamped by the family of Whites; the only place I felt safe and private was in my bedroom which was large and very cold. Sir Aubrey was solicitous and factual and fixed appointments with the doctor with whom they'd just registered. Lady Olivia fussed around and took away some of the caring that I would have liked to do myself. Viv lorded it over everyone. The two children were ghastly and crashed around without any discipline and I was cross when they invaded our bedroom at inconvenient moments. At the beginning of the visit, and regardless of the chaos, Peter sat in his chair in the kitchen, the only warm room in the house, and beamed at his family. He had not seen them all together for well over ten years. When his wounds began to scab he began to get edgy and wanted to exercise. I'd much rather have been alone with Peter and the only time that came about was bedtime. Peter's vulnerability in war and living in the rough and tumble of a family unit was affecting my thoughts about waiting for a baby. Badly behaved though Viv's children were they were a living symbol of her and her strange husband. I felt I needed some constant and continual evidence of our own union. I started to long for Peter to father a child.

"Peter," I said one night, not very long after we'd arrived.

"Yes, Emm. What's the matter? You sound so serious. Have you something up your sleeve?" He was in a jovial mood, responding to the attentions from those all around him.

"You know," I began, and faltered for words. "You know, you've become more precious to me since your flirtation with the bullet."

"Well, go on," he came and sat behind me on the bed, top button of his pyjamas undone, bandaged leg sticking out straight.

"I... er... I want something to remember you by for always, not just letters and memories."

"Yes?" He held my hand.

"I know I said I don't want a baby. Well, now I'd like to throw caution to the wind and try to get pregnant. Other people have babies and manage."

"Oh Emmy, I couldn't let you. All on your own. I'd be away most of the time." He took his hand away from mine and rubbed his forehead. "How would you manage. Do you really mean it?" He looked at me , his eyes penetrating deeply into mine.

"Of course I do. Shouldn't have suggested it otherwise. I REALLY REALLY want it. I'm very fit and well. Let's try this month." Then I laughed. "No more stupid tubes in the bath either."

"Be serious, Emm, are you sure?"

"Sure as I was when I knew you were the man for me." I was puzzled by Peter's cautious reaction.

Then Peter spoke, this time twisting round and holding both my hands. "You didn't realise, did you, that I'd wanted one from the start. But I had to go along with you as I saw your point of view. Best of all, I'd love a son. I don't know why, but I'd just love a son. There'll be yet another reason to get this damn war over." We lay back on the bed. We neither of us had anticipated any interference with our plan, but the heavy bandages, the sore wounds and stiff knee proved painful at most angles of love making. We both became quite giggly as we tried to manipulate ourselves into a suitable position. With patience, a lot of love and much trial and error we made ourselves comfortable and prayed for a son.

The four weeks went by all too quickly. Viv organised and tried to cook. She was a good organiser but a bad cook. In the afternoons Peter and I escaped from the house. He was anxious to exercise his leg. I was anxious to be free from domesticity.

One afternoon when walking briskly along the sand, with Peter only limping a little, he announced, "Must try to wheedle the old Doc to say I'm fit. Scabs are nearly off, and the leg's pretty strong. I've bccn away, nearly six

weeks, and that puts a lot of responsibility on the acting Company Commander."
I halted in my tracks and looked out to sea, my voice angry. "Why do you
have to be so urgent to get back? Why do you still have to prove your worth?
Why can't you realise that you're not indispensable?"

"Hey, hey," chided Peter. He stopped walking. "Strong words from a young
lady." There was a silence and Peter drew patterns in the sand with the toe of
his shoe. "Whatever you do or say, Emma, please don't send me away with a
sense of guilt. My gut feeling urges me on to get back. Be kind to me, darling.
I'm not really all that strong inside. Give me some sort of blessing. I don't want
to leave with the semblance of ill-will between us." He looked so young and
vulnerable with the wind tousling his hair, his shirt awry, his stick in his hand.
It wrung my heart to see the little boy in him.

"Darling, I adore you," and stood on tiptoe to kiss him. "Don't even think
of ill-will. It's just that I'll miss you."

"What about this stiff upper lip I'm always on about? You can do it, I know
you can." I could think of nothing to say, so held his arm and turned him
homewards.

It was six weeks from the day he arrived at the hospital that Peter was certi-
fied by the doctor that he was once again ready for battle. I suspect that the
doctor had been persuaded to speed things up but I never asked. Peter bought
a small wireless for his men, and packed up a big box of goodies. Together with
his old heavy rucksack which had been returned from the front, he looked
rather like a Christmas Tree with parcels and equipment sticking out all round.
There were cheerful farewells from the Whites, bravado prevailed, no tears, no
messages of endearment. I felt he might just as well be going on holiday. I
revelled in the thought that I had two nights with him alone, blissfully alone, in
the same London hotel that we had used before.

Saturday and Sunday were spent much as the last fleeting weekend we had,
walking, talking and eating well. When we strolled down the Mall, Peter still
limping very slightly, I willed people to look at us. I felt so proud. On our last
evening we had dinner at the Dorchester Hotel. The waiters flitted quietly and
efficiently attending to our needs, I wore the dress I was married in and felt
good. Peter looked handsome in his uniform which had just returned from the
cleaners. Sadly tension slowly rose between us.

Trying to be light hearted, I said laughing, "I remember the last time I came
here. My first night in England. And I wore my old school dress. I WAS
terrified." I recounted the story. When I got to the end I realised Peter wasn't
listening.

"I'm trying to make you laugh," I chided. "You've gone all serious again."

"I know. Every moment is so precious. Every glance you give me has a
thousand meanings. I want to remember... But I've thoughts of tomorrow
coming into my head clouding everything." He squashed up his napkin and

put it on his side plate. "Come on, darling. I want to take you to the hotel." He called for the bill and, with a faint raise of an eyebrow, he delved into his wallet for another note.

We didn't talk much as we walked arm in arm through St James' Park. The moon shone over the black roof tops, not a peep of light from any building. Without speaking, we went to our room, and once again we packed. There was another dawn start the following morning. Lovingly and with urgency we tried to fulfil our desire for a son.

While we were dressing in the dim dawn light Peter turned to me and said, "When you write to me with news that you're pregnant I'll be the proudest man in the world. Now we must both put our lives and trust in other people's hands."

"Don't get all solemn again," I brushed my hair unnecessarily hard. "I can't bear it when you are all serious, I'll walk with you to the Movements Office in Shaftesbury Avenue, then I'll come straight back here for breakfast. After that I'll go and see Aunt Mathilda. Its a pity she hasn't met you." Then I added in a harsher voice, though I didn't mean it to slip out, "I've got to, anyhow, haven't I?"

"Yes, you're right. We've all got to do these things. But, darling, thank you for marrying me. I only wish I could've made more of a home for you. You wait, Em, you wait till we can start properly together. I'll make you a queen." We laughed together a bit shakily.

We walked across St James ark, loaded with Peter's gear. It was so early in the morning that even the ducks were still asleep. The dew smelled sweet, the stars twinkled and slowly disappeared as the sun's rays crept across the sky.

When we arrived at the Movement Office we were confronted with two heavy swing doors. It said "Service Personnel only." "Look," Peter said firmly, "you wait here a tick, and I'll put the baggage just inside and find out where I'm to go. Then I'll come back and said good-bye." He disappeared through the swing doors.

I waited and waited biting my nails. Why doesn't he come back? I knew I couldn't wait outside the door forever. More and more people were arriving and were swallowed up by the revolving doors. I started to feel conspicuous just standing there. After an hour I despaired and left. Sorrowfully I walked back to the hotel across the park. It all seemed dead and desolate, very different from the moonlit or dawn walk. I ate a scanty breakfast and phoned Aunt Mathilda. She told me to come as soon as I could.

The welcome that the old lady showered on me brought back all my childhood memories. It also helped to quell the pain in my chest.

"My dear girl," she hugged me, took my coat, and settled me by her coal fire. "You look as if you've seen a ghost, Peter gone? Without saying goodbye? Something must have happened. Tell me about it. But first, look, this is your old cup, remember the crack?"

We sat over the cups of tea in front of the warm fire and words flowed from me. It was so different from the reserved feelings that I had to impose upon myself at Nairn. An afternoon with Aunt Mathilda, sharing my troubles, hearing her anxieties, talking about loneliness quite openly, helped me to lighten my heavy heart.

"But why am I adding to your troubles, Aunt Mathilda? I'm sure you're working too hard, you look as if you've seen two ghosts." She laughed her light infectious laugh, dabbing her nose with her tiny scented handkerchief.

"I'd like to die in harness," she replied. "I've never known what it is to rest. Being with the students keeps me in touch with what's going on. Otherwise we oldies get a bit cut off, shut away all day in our own houses."

"Wish you'd met Peter. I wish... Oh I wish I could curl up and go to sleep till it's all over." It was a wonderful sense of relief to be able to talk about defeat.

"I've had wishes like that when I was younger. When Charlie died I felt like dying too. But by the grace of someone, somewhere, we're given the strength to go on. You will be given the strength, darling, I'm sure you will be."

"Dear Aunt Mathilda. I feel I could talk to you forever. The Turnballs are lovely, and Di is my best friend, but you make me feel strong. I promise to bring Peter to see you next time we're in London, however short the visit." We talked away, often about my childhood days; the darkening skies and fading evening light made me realise that I had to get back to catch the deadly night train to Edinburgh and work.

"Goodbye dear. I'll keep you in my thoughts." Aunt Mathilda did not offer to walk to the station with me. She stood at her little wicket gate, old, fragile, but defiant.

I found a corner. A young sailor sat beside me. When he'd finished chewing his gum he fell asleep sitting upright, leaning right across my shoulders. I tried to push him upright again. In the end I found it easier to put my arms round him and rest my head on his. I laughed at the strange bedfellows that war brought about, and wondered what Peter would think if he saw me asleep with my arms round an able seaman.

Three days later a letter arrived from Peter. It was scribbled on a page torn from his pocket note book, and stuffed in a dirty old envelope.

"Darling, what can you think of me? I wasn't able to return to say goodbye. The thought haunts me. We were diverted down different corridors and there was no turning back. Forgive me, and try to understand. I am writing on the ferry, and will get a seaman to post it on his return. I hope he remembers. I wanted to tell you that I am so happy that you are my wife. That's all that really matters. Must fly. There's lots to do Peter." I tucked the note inside my shirt and read it again and again.

Back in the hospital I worked harder and harder. If there were any odd moments I would pop back into the military wards. The long term patients looked forward to my visits. Even Rusty looked up and smiled before he looked away.

One evening, two weeks after Peter had left, I returned to my tiny room with my back aching. My period had begun. I was distraught and depressed. I sat down to write to Peter.

December 19th, 1944

Darling, I've got a big disappointment for you. My periods have started and I'm not pregnant. I can hardly bear to tell you. I feel I've failed you. If I had returned from India sooner we might've managed it. I'm sure this will be a big set-back for you, and I'm so sorry, The world sometimes seems a hostile and unfriendly place. I've tried to give you all that I could of myself, yet this has happened. Forgive me, for I'm sure the fault is mine. But do go on taking care, remember I'm here waiting for you and the days when we can be together again. I will write another time. I'm too sad at the moment.

Emmy.

PS This will probably reach you about Christmas. But my small parcel and other letters with Christmas messages should certainly get to you before then.

Christmas came and went. I felt little emotion, little elation. The news that the British forces were advancing well into Burma, that my parents were happy and hopeful, had no effect. I could hear in my head the pounding of the guns, the squelching of boots in the mud, the coughing in the trenches. The nurses worked extra hours putting up decorations and wrapping small parcels. The men wanted to be back in their homes with their families. Sadly the oldies were often too senile to realise there was a difference in their daily routine.

On the second day of January 1945, a letter arrived from Peter. It was in a scruffy envelope with a Field Post Office stamp mark. I put it in my pocket and read it walking slowly in the frosty air in the hospital grounds.

My darling girl,

You mustn't worry about the baby. 'Course I'm disappointed, but we both did our best, and we'll make up for it soon. I was sad to miss Christmas with you, I think of you every day. I wish you were happier in your job. At least it's getting better than it was at the beginning.

We are even more in the thick of it, so letters will be spasmodic. I'm writing in the cellar of an old school. There's one bulb in the middle of the room, and we're all crowding under it for light. This is war in all it's ghastliness. I shall be glad when it's over. I could write and write about my feelings, about shelling beautiful buildings, about leaving small children hurt by the roadside and so on. When training, we don't see the reality of it all. But at last I'm doing what I set out to do, and hope I'm keeping my men as safe and well as possible.

On Christmas night there was an unspoken truce. Our men and the German soldiers all met in no man's land and drank a toast together. It was a strange and beautiful moment. Next morning they were fighting again. There is no animosity between soldier and soldier, it is the orders that they, and we, have to obey. Tonight I fear another attack is about to happen. Luckily I feel well, the old leg is no bother. We are all tired, but somehow somewhere comes that extra spark that keeps us going. My men are wonderful, and put up with the mud and cold. My, it's been cold. But the mud is our main enemy this side of the front line.

My precious girl, my eyes are closing. YOU are MY world, and one day I will prove it to you. Will write as often as I can. You are always in my thoughts, and that small photo is in constant use.

Your Peter.

Peter in the centre in January 1945

I plodded on at the hospital. Letters from Shillong came spasmodically. They were too on the fringes of the frantic mud and malaria-ridden battle for Burma. My days in Shillong seemed a different world. I wrote as cheerfully as I could to Clive and Ethel, told them a little about Peter's conditions but a lot about the wonderful month we had spent together in Nairn in the family house. In the first week of February the whole course of my life changed. I had done the rounds of the wards and I went back to my office. There was a note from Matron which asked me to go to her office as soon as possible.

I walked along the shiny polished corridor and knocked at the door. Matron was sitting at her desk.

"Don't worry Emma, don't worry. It's nothing worse than last time." Again I read the words, cold and clinical that had come in the orange-buff envelope. Peter had been 'slightly wounded'. It sounded the same as the previous message.

"Oh Matron," I said, feeling for a chair to sit on as my head began to swim. "When will it all end?"

Matron was as understanding as before. "I feel you young people must take hold of life as much as you can. We can always manage to cover your work. It is a bit more difficult with the nurses, but I usually manage."

"Thank you again. I'll let you know when I hear more about Peter. Must go and get packed and be ready to go wherever he is.

"Yes dear, you do just that. Try not to worry."

I left Matron sitting at her desk, and walked back to my bedroom. I packed my suitcase and tidied my drawers. I waited for the next telegram.

A week went by and I didn't hear. I realised I'd go mad if I didn't hear news soon. Previously the telegram had come within 48 hours. I didn't know who to contact. I spoke with two sergeants who had been in Peter's battalion, but not in his Company. They confirmed terrible fighting, confirmed there were officer casualties but couldn't give names. Two weeks passed, and I began to feel sick. I wondered where he was and what was the matter with him. I unpacked and packed my suitcase over and over again. Three weeks went by. I couldn't sleep, I couldn't eat. There was no reply to any of my letters. There was nothing at all.

I was sitting at my desk on that dark afternoon at the end of February, trying to read documents. The letters danced before my eyes. The porter knocked at the door. "Matron would like to see you, straight away." That was all he said.

I walked hoping against hope that it was news of Peter but something stopped me hurrying. I walked so slowly along the red tiled corridor. Matron stood in the window with another orange-buff envelope in her hand. I waited for her to speak.

"Shut the door Emma, and sit down."

"You've news for me Matron. I can see from your telegram. He's only slightly wounded. I'm all packed and ready to go. Which hospital am I to go to, Matron? Tell me, I'm getting all excited." I was out of breath with anticipation, my fingers drummed on the desk. I couldn't see the look on Matron's face.

"No dear," said Matron. "There'll be no journey to meet him. I'll read you the telegram. You must sit and be very brave. It reads like this. "War Office regret to inform you Major Peter White killed in action on 15th February 1945. Previous telegram sent in error. Major P White of the Canadian Forces was slightly wounded. Please accept apologies. Further information to follow."

The room started to whirl round me, I hung on to the desk. "It can't be Peter. It can't be. What are you telling me, Matron? I'm ready to go and meet him. I've been writing to him."

Matron passed me the telegram, putting her hand on my shoulder. The words blurred before my eyes. "You stay here for a while. I'll get a cup of tea. Use the phone if you need." There were no tears, no drama, just dull hurting pain. I heard Peter's voice saying that I was to be brave, not to cry. Blood pumped in my head, my brain was numb. On automatic action I dialled the Whites at Nairn; I had to dial twice my eyes were so clouded. Sir Aubrey answered. I stuttered out the message, reading from the telegram. He cried openly into the phone. "You poor child, you poor child," he kept on repeating. "Come up here as soon as you can."

Matron returned with the coffee. "I've telephoned Peter's parents and they think it'd be a good thing if I went to see them," I explained.

"That's the best thing you could do," she replied. "You're all packed so it won't take any time. I'll arrange a car to be at the Nurses Home in half an hour. It'll take you straight to the station. Phone your family again when you've looked up the trains. It's going to be a hard time lass, but you'll pull through . Don't be afraid of tears, Emma, they sometimes help."

"Can't do that Matron. Promised I wouldn't. Thank you for fixing the car. I'll let you know. Good-bye. Thank..." No more words would come out. My lips, throat, and breathing all seemed paralysed, I functioned automatically. I went to collect my packed suitcase, and was ready for the transport when it arrived. I saw no-one. The driver knew what had happened and drove without speaking straight to the station. I saw nothing out of the window, my thoughts were focused inward. I shut the door of the car and moved off without giving the driver a word of thanks.

When I went to buy my ticket I found I had no money. I had left my cheque book in a drawer. The banks were already closed. My brain was very tired, but I knew I was on my way to Nairn and needed cash. I wished the ache in my throat would go, and that my heart would stop thumping. I needed someone to look after me, and in a croaking voice I called out, "Peter, where are you?" A man passed by me and gave me a strange look. Then I told myself to pull myself together, and get myself out of a fix. With a stroke of good fortune I remembered Peter's tailors who were just around the corner and I decided to try them for a loan.

I walked down the small back street and found the little shop front. Inside were rolls and rolls of cloth and a lovely tweedy smell. The two brothers had tailored suits for the whole White family for generations. They both looked the same with shining silver hair and bushy eyebrows. Both were immaculately dressed.

"Well madam, it's nice to see you again," said the younger of the two brothers, who was well into his sixties himself. "And how's the Major? We heard of his wound before Christmas. His jacket will be ready for him when he's next on leave."

I was silent. I could not make myself formulate the words to say that Peter was dead. I didn't know how to say it. I felt like a twig snapped off a tree at the mercy of the elements.

"Is there anything I can do?" asked the older brother conscious of my silence.

"Yes there is." Then I spoke with a rush, words flowing with no stopping. I repeated, "Yes there is. I've just heard my husband has been killed and I'm trying to get to Nairn, and I've left my cheque book behind and I haven't enough money to buy the ticket and I thought I could come to ask you if you could lend me the money for the fare." I looked at the floor and waited.

"Oh, madam," they both said in unison. "I didn't know," said the younger brother. "Of course we'll help," said the older man. "Known the Major since he was a nipper, a right fine bairn. It's always the best that are taken." He turned towards the till and put some notes into an envelope. "Return it when you like, m'dear. Glad to be of help to the family. God bless you." The older man took a handkerchief from his pocket and blew his nose hard. The younger brother opened the door for me. "Goodbye madam. Take care of yourself. The Major would sure want that." The kindness of these two men threatened to break down my outward self-composure. I managed to wave my hand in farewell.

I bought a single ticket to Nairn, and sat in the first corner seat I could find. Thoughts and memories swept over me. In my mind I talked to Peter, asked him questions. "What shall I do, my beloved? I just don't know what to do. I'd planned to be with you, waiting for you, longing for you. Now they say you're dead. You've been taken away. Where shall I go? I don't want to live in Nairn forever. Will I always have to struggle to be brave, to care for other people? Who'll care for me?" All of a sudden I felt exhaustion and despair sweep over me like the rough waves on a beach, pounding and retreating, pounding and retreating. The rest of the beach was a big black hole. I got to the toilet for a wash to see if I could rid myself of the blackness. Nothing helped. Then I stood by the carriage door and looked out of the window. Dark thoughts flashed through my mind. Nobody would miss me, nobody would see me. Another train would come along and that would be that. Then I seemed to see Peter in the distance, I could go and be with Peter forever, I felt calm... I fumbled with the lock of the door, but it was stiff. I kicked the door with my foot, but it was stiff. I kicked the door with my foot, but I couldn't open it. Then something seemed to speak to me, not to my mind, my body or my spirit. I felt rather than heard the words, "Come on Emma. There's life before you. Remember Peter. He wants you to stay around."

"Heavens, what's happening to me?" I murmured out loud.

"Don't worry, Miss, don't worry. Taken a bit queer you were. I were on my rounds and saw you. You just sit down for a while." The guard led me to my seat and sat me down. He did not speak again, but hovered round the corridor and kept on looking at me to see if I'd recovered. I wondered what had happened to me, and who it was that spoke to me about Peter. I felt I was in the hands of someone else. Was this a form of God speaking to me? Did this stop me from jumping out? I'll never know. All I knew was I'd got to face this damn world squarely with only Peter's memory to help.

The greeting at Nairn was sombre but loving. Sir Aubrey found it hard to control his tears. Lady Olivia walked about as if in a trance. It was Viv who kept the wheels of the household functioning. I could see why Peter had thought so much of his sister. She was, indeed, a strong person. Movement and activity helped to swamp the pain, but at night it returned, worse than ever. I slept in the bed that we had shared and wept silently into the pillow.

After a week in Nairn I received a letter from Melville which had been forwarded from the hospital.

Dear Mrs White,

I felt I had to write to you about the Major. I heard there was a terrible muddle. Can't believe it. There was another Major White, a Canadian, wounded on the same day. He was sent back to the UK. Don't know more about him. The telegrams got crossed. We are all so sorry about it. The Major was a wonderful man to be with. He got another wound in the thigh trying to deliver a message across an open area. It was very exposed. He knew it would be dangerous. I saw him that evening in the Casualty Clearing Station, very cheerful he was, though angry at being out of action again. When I went the next morning I was told he had died in the night for loss of blood. He had told the medical staff to look after the others as his wound was only slight. But he bled to death. It all could've been avoided. We miss him. He was so well liked. Please accept my sympathy, Mrs White. I've lost a good and respected friend, and the Battalion has lost one of its finest officers.

I am, respectfully yours, Adrian Melville.

I showed the letter to the Whites and walked out of the room. I had nothing to say. Other letters poured in. They were of no help, but gave me something more to do. I felt my answers were all so false; I couldn't write off my pain, my anger, my confusion. I really didn't feel like doing anything anymore. I couldn't be bothered. Once I heard the family say "What shall we do with Emma" I really didn't care what they did with Emma. Then a letter came from Ethel. She suggested that I should return to Shillong and join up with the Burma Army till that campaign had finished. The idea fell on me like a flat fish, I just didn't care. I wanted to stay in Nairn, and I didn't want to go back to Assam and be a little girl again. I left my life in the hands of others to make any decisions as to what to do with Emma.

Sir Aubrey managed to pull a few strings in the shipping world and a berth was arranged for me to return to India in early May. I felt like a parcel being dispatched. I couldn't care.

In the weeks before I sailed I was organised to make many journeys. The first one was to the hospital where I collected my things and said good bye to the long stay patients. I felt safer now when I was given condolences and knew that other people were more embarrassed to talk about death on active service than I was. I popped in to see Rusty, and was delighted to see him up and about. He was able to recognise me and shake me by the hand.

Then I went to Matron's office and sat once again in the same chair where I heard the fateful news. "You've been a great help to me, Matron. Thank you for everything." But that damn lump in my throat started to rise again, and I couldn't speak any further.

Matron led me to the door with her arm round my shoulder. "Take care of yourself, Emma. You're strong enough to ride the rough times. I hope for your sake you find another man. Good-bye my dear." She gently shoved me down the corridor, I blessed her for her understanding.

Then I made a final trip to London to see Di, her family, and Aunt Mathilda. Di was brusque and outwardly unsympathetic. We promised to write. Mrs Turnball cried softly into her handkerchief, offered me her home whenever I needed it. Mr Turnball looked out of the window, ramrod stiff; it was as if he was not able to hear of any more distress. It was the same with Aunt Mathilda, more loving words, more tears.

"Leave a little room in your heart for me," said the old lady. "I wish I could carry some of your pain." She tucked my hands into her old gnarled ones and carried them to her lips. She turned away without kissing me and walked back down her small path. I paused and looked at the little house, hoping for some comfort, but there was none. I hoped they realised that I loved them all, but just wasn't strong enough to show anything at this moment. In a queer way I longed for the boat when I knew I'd have time and space to sort myself out. There was further strain when the day of departure from Nairn approached. No one really wanted me to go as I was a physical link with Peter, their son. But it had to be, and tearless with straight-faced stoicism they helped me and all my worldly possessions on to the train for Glasgow and stood waving till I was out of sight.

The SS Albatross was very different from the SS Terne and the troopship. The ship was manned by a Dutch crew. Everything sparkled. Everything was clean. I had a cabin to myself. There were only twenty other passengers, the cargo took up most of the space. The officers all spoke English and looked disciplined and tidy. None of them had been back to their native Holland for five years. The German occupation and the Allied invasion made them fear for their families.

The ship was still blacked out, but trouble from U-boats had rescinded. The Allied forces on the Western front looked near to victory. The Albatross was able to sail through the Mediterranean. I tried hard to join in with the talking, the drinking, the general bonhomie, but I spent much of my time on the upper deck leaning against the rails. I had sailed for England with so much hope. I was returning with nothing. It was wonderfully soothing to be battered with spray, or just watch the phosphorescence by night and the flying fish by day. I wished I could share the red glow of the sunset, slowly disappearing behind the horizon with… Sharply I steered my thoughts away from things I couldn't have. I wasn't able to relax with the other passengers, the general bonhomie was false, their drinking habits obscene.

Night after night I left the drinking merry-making and leant on the railings on the top deck, sometimes crying quietly. Night after night a Dutch sailor, dark-haired and brown-eyed, walked past along the deck. He looked at me closely; but he never spoke.

In early June the ship was a hive of excitement with the news of the end of the war. Champagne and wine flowed in the dining saloon. The Dutch crew were delighted at the thought that they could at last be re-united with their families. Again I slipped out to the top deck. Again the young Dutch sailor paced by. The moon was high in the sky and I could see his young face etched with lines of weariness. I felt sad for him.

"Good news for you," I said as he came on his third round.

He seemed glad to stop to talk. "Good news for us lot," he commented, "But it didn't end soon enough for you both, did it?" he asked gently, leaning his arms on the railings and looking across the moon patterned water.

"How did you know?"

"News travels fast on a small ship. It must be even harder for you to hear all the celebrating. We're all able to feel we can go back now." He paused and looked out to sea with accustomed eyes. I didn't feel like adding to the conversation yet, so he continued. "It's been a long time, you know, for everyone without seeing their families. It's a bit different for me." He looked down at his feet and drew lines in the dampness on the wooden deck. "My wife and child… Well, they were killed in the early bombing back in 1941." I drew in my breath and wished he'd not told me. "It's a long time now, and the years've put things into perspective." Then he looked at me directly. "You don't mind if I talk to you, do you? I've seen you here most evenings, on your own."

I still said nothing, waves of uncertainty sweeping across me.

Taking my silence as a permission he continued, "Don't like all that drinking either. When I'm out of this uniform, I'll go back to the land. That's really where I belong…" He looked at me again.

"I can't believe you're Dutch," I said.

"Mother was English. I went to a boarding school in Surrey. But Father was Dutch, he was very upset, when I didn't, no wouldn't, take a commission."

"Oh! Is that why you don't have rings round your cuff?"

"Yes," laughed the young man. "And I don't have to go in to the main dining saloon and spend hours drinking and eating. The seamen's Mess is a bit rough, but much more relaxed."

I started to feel I could converse with this different sort of person.

Together in silence, we walked to the rails and leant over and together we watched the movement of the sea swelling up and down, up and down. The bows of the ship cut a curling arc of phosphorescent foam, shining and smooth, shining and smooth. There was a continuity in the movement, reassuring, reassuring, reassuring.

The cemetary in Kohima

Emma in 1945 after Peter's death

B Coy. 7 Bn, Summer 1944 at Comrie, Perthshire

The survivors